You Are Wha

Make Yourself To Be

THE STORY OF A
VICTORIAN ABORIGINAL FAMILY
1842–1980

PHILLIP PEPPER
with
TESS DE ARAUGO

HYLAND HOUSE   MELBOURNE

Dedicated   **TO MY PEOPLE**

*Without the assistance of my friend and researcher,
Tess De Araugo, I wouldn't have been able to put
together this book about my family and people.*

Phillip Pepper

TO MY FRIENDS
ETHEL AND PHILLIP

In preparing this edition you are with me once more.

Tess De Araugo

Title page: **Tribal Aborigines known as Queen Lily and King Billy of Ramahyuck,
1860s. Lily died of consumption in 1886 aged 54** (Stratford Historical Society).

First published 1980 by
Hyland House Publishing Pty Limited
10 Hyland Street
South Yarra
Melbourne
Victoria 3141
Revised edition 1989

Pepper, Phillip.
    You are what you make yourself to be.

New ed.
ISBN 0 947062 60 2.

1. Pepper family. [2]. Aborigines, Australian—Vi◄
—Biography. I. De Araugo, Tess. II. Title.

929.209945

Edited by Tess De Araugo
Designed by Robin Cowpe
Typeset by Solo Typesetting.
South Australia
Printed by Globe Press Pty Ltd.
50 Weston Street, Brunswick

Foreword

THIS BOOK IS THE RESULT OF A FRUITFUL COLLABORATION BETWEEN THE author, Phillip Pepper, and Tess De Araugo, his researcher and friend who was taken on visits by Phillip Pepper to places of Aboriginal significance in Victoria. He told her in conversations and taped messages about his family and his own experiences. Library research followed for Tess De Araugo, but the book highlights the reminiscences of Phillip Pepper, a distinguished Gippsland Aboriginal.

The book provides a much-needed Aboriginal viewpoint on the history of Aboriginal/European relations in Gippsland during the long lifetime of Mr Pepper. But it extends beyond his 72 years, thanks to his ability to recall information passed on to him by Aborigines long since dead. These old people rarely confided in persons other than members of their own race and we must be grateful to have their stories committed to print at last. This is an important book, the first ever written by a Gippsland Aboriginal; fortunately it will be added to a small but growing number of such Aboriginal publications.

I first met Mr Pepper in 1966 when he made a number of visits to Lake Tyers to encourage the residents there who were desperately contending with the Victorian Government's Aborigines Welfare Board to retain the reserve as an Aboriginal community. The struggle was between a powerful Board determined to disperse families from Lake Tyers as quickly as possible, and relatively powerless Aboriginal families wanting to retain the security of some 4000 acres of land which they regarded as their own. The people needed every encouragement in those traumatic days and Phillip Pepper did what he could in the circumstances. I remember him for his cheerful optimism and his store of jokes and anecdotes. It came as no surprise to me that Mr Pepper should have chosen the title of this book as he did. 'You are what you make yourself to be' sums up the man's outlook very well.

Mr Pepper is a descendant of Aborigines who were thrust out of Gippsland Aboriginal communities as a result of the passage of brutal legislation in 1886. This obliged persons defined as 'half-castes' to leave reservations and to make their way as best they could, in isolation from kin, in the general Australian community. Mr Pepper's forebears were amongst those who survived and they appear to have passed on to him something of their fighting spirit. Another part of their legacy to him, one which is apparent in this book is a deep respect for kin and kinship obligations. This is an important factor in any Aboriginal society but has, more often than not, been disregarded or not understood in the administration of Aboriginal affairs in Victoria.

The Pepper story takes us through the last decades of the nineteenth century when the harsh 'half-caste' legislation first operated, and up to the 1960s and more recent years. Mr Pepper's treatment of these two recent turbulent decades, when so much happened in this State, is understandably incomplete. I am confident however that future historians will draw a parallel between the performance of the Aborigines Welfare Board in relation to Lake Tyers and the Board for the Protection of Aborigines who initiated the nineteenth-century legislation referred to above. Both Boards were possibly well-meaning; certainly both, in effect, struck at the sense of security and the kinship ties of Aborigines and created considerable physical and emotional suffering.

The Lake Tyers policies of the Aborigines Welfare Board were an example of history repeating itself. But the granting of title to the land at Lake Tyers to Aborigines in 1971, an event briefly referred to by Mr Pepper, was unprecedented in this State. With the perspective of time this granting of title will be seen in its true light as a most cynical exercise. At the same time it was a clever move. After all, who could criticise a government for granting Aborigines title to land, something the people themselves had demanded for a number of years?

The Aborigines Welfare Board went out of existence in 1968 unlamented, certainly by Aboriginal people. It was replaced by a full government department, the Ministry of Aboriginal Affairs, with a new permanent head. The previous Board failed in its attempt completely to depopulate the Lake Tyers reserve. The community there was a constant focal point of criticism for the government and a potential source of embarrassment for the new administration. So it was decided to cut the millstone free and in this way to disclaim any future responsibility for events at Lake Tyers.

Self-determination, land title and the privilege of working a few hundred acres of poorly-developed farm land were granted to the Aboriginal families. This was done to a people who as recently as 1966 had existed under crude authority on a hand-out system of rations and pocket money, and lived in tiny inadequate huts without bathrooms, proper stoves, running water or electricity.

The people of Lake Tyers survived 100 years of authoritarian management, and they survived the dispersal attempts of the 1880s and the 1960s, but this move was to bring them to their knees.

The community still struggles on crushed under the weight of events over which they have had little or no control. Not for the Lake Tyers people to say 'You are what you make yourself to be'. Not yet, but such is the resilience of the human spirit that possibly there is hope. Phillip Pepper, I am sure, would believe there was.

Alan West,
Melbourne

4

Contents

Acknowledgements

The author's and researcher's special thanks to Mr Alan West, Curator in Anthropology, National Museum of Victoria and the staff; Miss Sue McKemmish and staff at the Australian Archives, Melbourne; staff at the La Trobe Collection, State Library of Victoria; the Public Record Office of Victoria; the Avon Shire Council; the Committee of Management of the Ramahyuck Cemetery; the Australian Heritage Commission; the Bairnsdale, Dandenong, Horsham, Koo-wee-rup Swamp, Maffra and District, Nihill, Sale and District, Tambo Shire, Warracknabeal, Yarram and District and especially the Stratford and District Historical Societies; to the editors of the *Bairnsdale Advertiser* and *Snowy River Mail*; to Geoff Hahn and Laurie Hamlyn for information on Ramahyuck; to T. Burhop, Father Joseph Butscher, N. Cochrane, Dr J. Flood, J. Hahn and J. L. Sala.

Our thanks are due also to the many kind people who have donated material and valuable information for this book and the two larger volumes to be published, *What Did Happen to the Aborigines of Victoria*. These people and organisations will be acknowledged fully in the relevant volumes. So many old letters, diaries, press clippings, photographs and post-cards remain packed away in boxes and cases which are almost forgotten. We would appreciate having access to them and the use of them, for publication in further stories about the Aborigines of Victoria and the early history of this state.

The author sincerely thanks the Aboriginal Arts Board of the Australia Council for the assistance with a grant which has made possible the publication of this book.

Phillip Pepper would like to thank Tess and Maurie for the time and work they have spent on helping with this book, and his wife Ethel for having tolerance and patience with him and for her help and guidance.

Tess De Araugo: without the co-operation of my husband and children in family affairs and Aboriginal Affairs my work with Phillip would be unfinished as far as this book is concerned. I look confidently forward to their continued support in the writing projects already well underway with Phillip and Ethel.

Introduction

Phillip Pepper, 1980.

PHILLIP PEPPER WAS BORN IN GIPPSLAND, VICTORIA, IN 1907 AND, APART from a short time working in New South Wales and Melbourne, he has lived in Gippsland all his life. Phillip has been an active member of the Aboriginal Affairs Advisory Council and the Aboriginal Lands Council, both of which are now terminated. He has been a friend, advisor and counsellor to his people; a humorist and a peace-lover. Phillip married Ethel Thomas in 1928 and they have one daughter and two sons, nine grandchildren and six great grandchildren.

Concern regarding the history of the Aborigines of Victoria — his people — prompted him to record his own immediate family history and the stories and legends passed down to him. Phillip asked, 'How will our grandchildren and our great grandchildren know about the way our ancestors lived if I don't leave something for them to look at?'

Phillip Pepper's father's people belonged to the Wotjoballuk nation in the Wimmera district of north-western Victoria and his mother's people were members of the vast Kurnai nation of Gippsland. Tracing their lives revealed a phase in the history of Victoria too startling to be ignored, and Phillip suggested we gather the facts and present them to 'our people'. In doing so, we compiled a history of the Aborigines' first contacts with the white race in Victoria and from this we extract now Phillip's own family story, which he has named *You Are What You Make Yourself To Be*. This is the companion to a general history entitled *What Did Happen to the Aborigines of Victoria*, of which Volume 1, *The Kurnai of Gippsland*, has been published.

Through these works, Phillip believes, an awareness and understanding will be promoted of the lives the Aborigines were compelled to follow under white authority in all its forms from convict shepherd to Governor. His wish is that this knowledge will assist the dark people and the white to take into consideration the past, in all its aspects, when looking at the present and the future and what that holds for his people. He hopes for peace and understanding, dignity and the confidence to believe that you are what you make yourself to be.

June 1980   *Tess De Araugo*,
                                                                                      Melbourne

Introduction to the Second Edition

Ethel died in 1984 and without her, his best friend and long time companion, Phillip lost all desire to live. He found his peace less than twelve months later. Phillip Pepper left an impression on all those who knew him that will never fade.

September 1989   *Tess De Araugo*,
                                                                                        Rosebud

Nathaniel of the Wotjoballuk Tribe

Nathaniel Pepper about 1868

YOU SEE MY GRANDFATHER WAS THE FIRST TRIBAL ABORIGINAL PERSON TO be baptised in Victoria; probably in the whole of Australia. His name was Nathaniel Pepper and he lived in the Wimmera out at Ebenezer, a mission there, and he married a girl who came from Western Australia somewhere. I'd like to know more about that. Anyway, he came down to Gippsland after a while because she died, and he came to Ramahyuck with Rev. Hagenauer. We often talked about Nathaniel Pepper and how we come to be called Pepper.

I'm getting up in years now, and there are a lot of things I know that nobody else knows about, and I'd like it to be written down because that never gets lost. If you talk it to people they forget it.

People come and ask our people about what happened in the past, and they ask us how we are living now and they ask about the health of our people and our housing problems and about our buried people—sometimes they want to dig them up and put them somewhere else. But then we never hear anything back. Sometimes the students come and ask questions to write a book or for something to do with their education and we never hear anything of them again.

And so I think it's time that we put it all down, all of what we remember: everything Ethel's father and my grandfather Billy Thorpe told us about the early days in Gippsland too. Nathaniel died young but his people, and their stories, some of it came to us. There's a lot I'd like to find out as well.

One time when I talked to my old grandfather Billy Thorpe in Gippsland, I asked him about the things that happened—things I'd been told like people put chains on the blackfellas in the first place, the white people when they came here, and other things. I wanted to know about a bloke that got speared at Orbost—and he said to me, 'Willie'—he used to call me Willie 'cos me second name's Willie—'Willie' he said, 'the *lohans** are here to stay. We have to learn to live with them. No good bringing back all the things that happened in the early days. What's the good of that? Makes people not nice with each other, talking about it all again. It's much better for us to try and forget those things because the *lohans* have come here to our country and they're not gonna go away. So the only thing for us to do is get on with them the best we can. Doesn't do any good talking about the things that happened, Willie.' But I said, 'Granpa one day I might want to know the truth about the things I hear—one time other people might want to know.' When I got older Grandfather did tell me things, some of them funny, some of them aren't. These are the things I want to put down.

* 'Lohan' is the Kurnai word for white man.

We learnt Aboriginal words, you know—sentences too. I know a lot but I don't talk about that business because people would only laugh. Even our own grandchildren haven't heard us talk our language. I'm forgetting it now, but there are still some words I remember. Ethel does too. But I want them written down.

When the white people came they couldn't say our Aboriginal names and a lot of the Aborigines, those tribal fellas, they took the name of whoever white blokes come on to their land or the white people gave them the name, or any name that come into their head, and it stuck to them. You don't know how Nathaniel got Pepper. There must have been some white bloke up there somewhere. It would be good if you could find out all about Nathaniel Pepper and his people—our history.

Nathaniel was a full-blood and so was the girl he married at Antwerp. Her name was Rachel, but they didn't have any children that lived. Nathaniel had brothers and we've got relations there now and when my Dad was young he used to go and stay with them. Well I don't know how you'd find out but I want you to find out for me all about them if you can. When Nathaniel was a young man he lived on the Ebenezer Mission near Antwerp. That could be a start. Rev. Hagenauer had a lot to do with him. He was there when Nathaniel was at that mission. When Rev. Hagenauer went to Gippsland the old people called him *moongan* and his wife was *yuccan*, the Gippsland language for father and mother.

We discovered that Rev. F. Hagenauer was a missionary of the Moravian Brethren, a Christian sect originating in Bohemia which later moved to Germany.

Rev. Hagenauer arrived in Melbourne in 1858, not quite thirty years old, to begin his work among the Aborigines of Victoria. He was accompanied by a fellow-Moravian, Rev. Spieseke. After they had taken part in an enquiry into the conditions of the Aborigines it was decided the two men were needed most in the Wimmera district of north-west Victoria where the discovery of gold had caused additional hardships for the tribes.

Rev. F. Hagenauer and his wife, 1908.

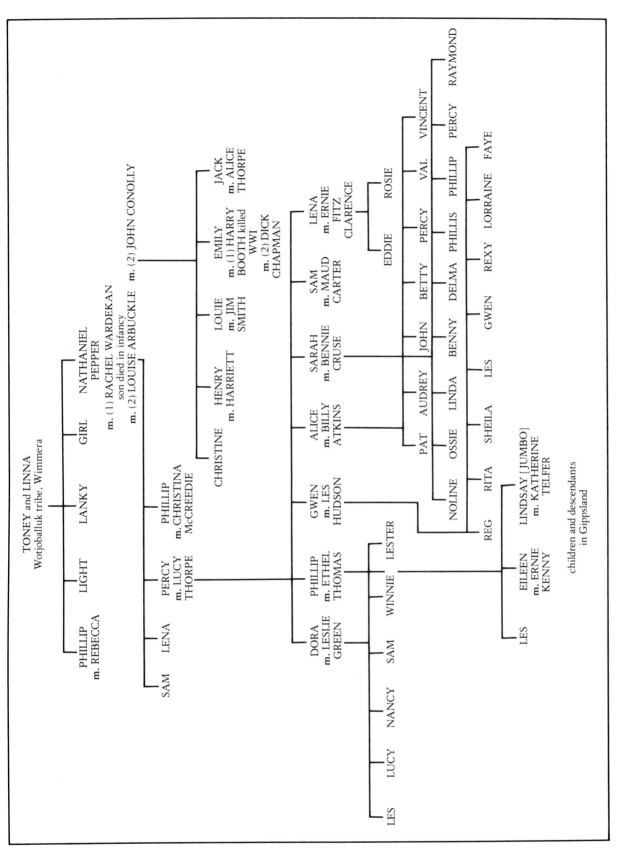

TONEY and LINNA
Wotjoballuk tribe, Wimmera

PHILLIP
m. REBECCA

LIGHT

LANKY

GIRL

NATHANIEL
PEPPER

m. (1) RACHEL WARDEKAN
son died in infancy
m. (2) LOUISE ARBUCKLE   m. (2) JOHN CONOLLY

SAM

LENA

PERCY
m. LUCY
THORPE

PHILLIP
m. CHRISTINA
McCREEDIE

CHRISTINE

HENRY
m. HARRIETT

LOUIE
m. JIM
SMITH

EMILY
m. (1) HARRY
BOOTH killed
WWI
m. (2) DICK
CHAPMAN

JACK
m. ALICE
THORPE

DORA
m. LESLIE
GREEN

PHILLIP
m. ETHEL
THOMAS

GWEN
m. LES
HUDSON

ALICE
m. BILLY
ATKINS

SARAH
m. BENNIE
CRUSE

SAM
m. MAUD
CARTER

LENA
m. ERNIE
FITZ
CLARENCE

LES

LUCY

NANCY

SAM

WINNIE

LESTER

REG

NOLINE

PAT

AUDREY

JOHN

EDDIE

ROSIE

BETTY

PERCY

VAL

VINCENT

OSSIE

LINDA

BENNY

DELMA

PHILLIS

PERCY

RAYMOND

RITA

SHEILA

LES

GWEN

REXY

LORRAINE

FAYE

EILEEN
m. ERNIE
KENNY

LINDSAY [JUMBO]
m. KATHERINE
TELFER

LES

children and descendants
in Gippsland

11

In Christmas week 1858 the Germans chose a site to develop the station on, land near the Wimmera River. They were guests at Ellerman's station, Antwerp, north of Dimboola, while they prepared a hut to live in and the first tribal boys they met at Antwerp were known as Pepper and Boney.[1]

Things were crook for the Aborigines when gold was discovered — caused trouble for our people where ever it was found. That camp site where they started the mission was Ebenezer. My people were still living their tribal life when Rev. Hagenauer went there. The white blokes had a lot of the land there because they were squashed out of down further. That's when the trouble started for my ancestors in that district.

The bad times really started when that fella Batman come into Melbourne. It was then the Aborigines around that area had a pretty hard time of it.

The Aborigines of Port Phillip saw the first exploration party from Launceston in 1835. An Irishman, Andrew Todd, with seven Sydney Aborigines and two white men remained at Indented Head for six weeks and established a depot, while John Batman returned to Launceston.

Andrew Todd's wife said her husband 'drew up the document between Mr Batman and the blacks for the purchase of lands'. Todd had asked the leader of the tribesmen of the Yarra* to make his mark on a tree and, when this was done, Todd copied the mark on to the document, just as Batman had ordered.[2]

When the men of John Pascoe Fawkner's opposition exploring party were discovered squatting on Batman's chosen site near the river, Henry Batman, John's brother, relayed instructions issued by Batman 'to expel any intruders by force or to induce the natives to attack them'.[3]

A long-drawn-out argument began over who was the first discoverer of the new settlement which was called Beargrass until Governor Bourke renamed it Melbourne in 1837.[4]

When Joseph Gellibrand, ex-attorney-general of Van Diemen's Land and a member of the Port Phillip Association, was at Beargrass in 1836 his 'association with the natives was on a friendly footing and the natives had the best of feelings towards the whites'. At that time there were about eight hundred Aborigines in the Beargrass district. The population of the white people was less than two hundred. At Indented Head Gellibrand discovered the tribes 'who were most peaceably disposed' had all departed; men at the station had threatened to shoot them because they had bandicooted† the potatoes. Gellibrand said 'the threats had been made use of without the slightest intention of carrying them into execution'.[5]

When Captain Lonsdale's administration of Beargrass commenced in 1836 the government was anxious to maintain a friendly association with the Aborigines and he was to induce them to offer their labour in return for food and clothing.[6]

They were made subject to the laws of England, it was said for their own protection, but those laws must equally operate for their restraint or punishment if they offended the white people — 'They must accordingly be sent to Sydney for trial if they commit a crime of such magnitude as to require it.'[7]

---

* The tribesmen referred to part of the river as Barrem, but the Sydney Aborigines called it Yarra Yarra.
† Removed the potatoes and replaced the plant.

In 1839 the British government, horrified by reports of the treatment the Australian Aborigines were receiving, formed a Protectorate* for the Port Phillip District, consisting of a Chief Protector and four assistants who were based in various parts of the colony.[8]

I never knew anything about those Protectors of the Aborigines. I do know a lot of things were done to the Aborigines, but around Melbourne area I don't know what happened there. The stories are it was pretty crook for them. A lot of the men who came to Victoria in those days come from Tasmania and you know what happened to the Tasmanian Aborigines, don't you?

Y'know they called us—what you call it—savages, yes, savages they said we were, our people. The boot was on the other foot you know. Look at what they did to our people. And we had no terrible diseases either till those convicts and settlers come here; no measles or anything.

A continuous stream of men deserted their ships in port and made their way to the land-holders' runs, where many preferred working as splitters because the timber was in great demand. The men had huts provided for them, usually miles from the main house, and the Aborigines were easy prey: 'when a native girl was captured by a white man and he had satisfied his brutal lust he very often promised her people better conditions', such as food or guns for their own protection. 'When he did not keep his word with the natives he paid with his life.'

Forced association of the women with the white men introduced venereal disease to the tribes. William Thomas, an Aboriginal Protector, said 'Natives old and young, even babies at the breast were infected with venereal disease. I have known hapless infants brought into this world, literally rotten with this disease.'

The Aborigines were in trouble in the occupied areas of Victoria, sometimes driven by sheer hunger to spear cattle or sheep as the white men and stock pushed further inland. La Trobe said, 'police arrangements should steadily keep pace with the occupation of the country by the settlers', and he appointed Henry Dana to form a Native Police Corps.[9]

Not much good they'd do. Our fellas wouldn't understand a word of their lingo. Aborigines from different areas had a language of their own, just like the Germans and French—same all over Australia. The whites didn't know what they were talking about either.

The Aborigines were hunted, poisoned, shot, left wounded, hung, drowned and flogged. Sometimes they were taken to Melbourne by the native police and their white officers for trial. The official body was often assisted by the settlers and their servants, who were usually convicts.

Many settlers made their way to the Wimmera River district. One of them was an Irishman, John Pepper, a young, wealthy and optimistic man who had left the family estate in northern Ireland to see the much-talked-about new colony. John Pepper had sheep but no land and when he reached the Wotjoballuk country he took up land near Lake Hindmarsh, Nhill and Pine Hills. Native food was plentiful when he moved in—black-faced kangaroos, wallabies, mallee fowl and birds. The lake supplied swans, pelicans, ducks

* See page 30.

and fish. John Pepper lived for eleven years in the Wotjoballuk territory in harmony with the Aborigines. The same could not be said for a number of the first squatters and their labourers in the Wimmera.

As the country was taken up quickly, the lives of the Wotjoballuk changed. The squatters said they stole their sheep and 'often formed parties to shoot down the blacks as it was a fight for life in many cases'. One of the Protectors instructed the Aborigines not to annoy the settlers in any way, but he was told 'since jumbucs come, they eat all the roots of food—only hungry black eat jumbuc—kangaroo have all gone—white fellas shoot too much blackfella . . . what for no put white fella in gaol?'

William Taylor at Longerenong on the Wimmera River and Yarriambiak Creek said, 'the natives were very troublesome during the winter'. When he first took up that run in February 1844 there were no Aborigines, but two months later about one hundred men, women and children 'came in . . . they were in the habit of stealing a sheep occasionally at night'. About five months later Taylor said there were forty natives on his land and spears were thrown at the shepherd and sheep were taken. The overseer mustered the men and the sheep were regained within an hour.

About the same time, sheep were missing from Horatio Ellerman's station, Antwerp, and a band of men set out after the tribesmen suspected of the theft. They found a group of Gromiluks in their camp on the banks of the Wimmera, where the river twisted in its course forming a shelter. The white men fired on the Aborigines and killed one of the women.

The limestone church at Ebenezer, opened 1875 (Miss Susan Robinson).

When the two Moravian missionaries began their work at Ebenezer, the majority of the Aborigines were suffering from consumption and skin diseases. The death rate was alarming and Rev. Spieseke said 'they are indeed upon their death beds' and he said there was a longing amongst them for a settled residence. Horatio Ellerman gave the missionaries one square mile of land in a bend of the Wimmera called Punyo Bunnutt by the Aborigines. There was an empty shepherd's hut not far away and Ellerman said they could use it for a school. One of the first pupils was a sixteen-year-old Gromiluk boy of the Wotjoballuk. He was called Pepper.

Pepper was four years old when John Pepper first grazed his sheep on the land where Pepper's family group had lived and, being in constant touch with white men, young Pepper had no language problems when he approached the Moravians. The Germans could only just speak understandable English, although Rev. Spieseke's English was a little more fluent than that of Rev. Hagenauer. It is quite possible that Pepper and his brother Charley were able to help the Germans with their language difficulties.

Pepper set to work building a bark hut for himself as soon as he decided to stay on the mission and not return to his group. His cousins Corny and Boney helped him with his hut.

As the time passed, Pepper learnt to read and write so well that he was able to help the missionaries teach his own people. By then most of his own large family had come to Ebenezer; his mother Linna, Toney his father, and brothers Charley, Lanky and Light, at least one sister, and his uncle and cousins. They all received religious instructions from the Moravians and, when Pepper knew enough about God and this new life he had learnt to love, he taught the Aborigines. Sometimes he left the mission, walking miles around the country giving instruction to his own people, teaching them to read and encouraging them to go to Ebenezer. Most of the Wotjoballuk living on the land taken up by the squatters were hopelessly ill.[10]

MISSIONARIES SAVED
ABORIGINES FROM EXTINCTION

Only for the missionaries there wouldn't be so many Aborigines walking around today. They're the ones that saved the day for us. Our people were finished before the mission men came. I'll tell you what upset the whole apple-cart. When the Europeans first come here they didn't know what a blackfella was. Old Hagenauer took them sick ones in and gave them medicine and food too. And they learnt to be Christian. Their tribal business was messed up before that. I mean their full tribal life, the culture.

Pepper was baptised and given the name of his own choice, Nathaniel. The ceremony was in August 1860, the day the new church at Ebenezer was consecrated. Almost two hundred white people gathered there to share the day with the Aborigines. The news that 'a native had actually been converted' created such a sensation in Melbourne that Rev. Hagenauer had to tell the story at a meeting where Nathaniel's friend Rev. Lloyd Chase gave detailed information about Nathaniel's character. In a way Rev. Chase had adopted Nathaniel's group, because some years earlier he had had one of the family living with him in Melbourne.[11]

Now you're talking about Willie, Nathaniel's cousin. A white Christian woman in Melbourne got a little book about Willie from England and that's how we found out about Willie in England. We didn't know about that overseas bit about him; only that there was terrible trouble with the farmers.

15

The Reverend Chase took Willie to England but he died there. His grave is still there and we tried to get a picture of it but we couldn't. And that Reverend come back and went up to Willie's place and met my grandfather Nathaniel. He knew Willie's father and brothers too. His other cousin, Charley, was baptised at Ebenezer and called Phillip. He was Nathaniel's brother. See how the old people passed the names on? They call me Phillip William.

Corroborees were still going on out in the bush. They were painted up and had the branches tied on their legs and all that. Trouble was, they were pretty sick and hungry and didn't have many places left to hunt their food and when there started to be a lot of pubs about, our people got the grog—'course they couldn't handle that. Our Christian blokes tried to get them away from it.

The Moravians heard rumours that Nine Creeks (Dimboola) was to have a public-house. In vain did magistrates, ministers and the Honorary Guardians object.* The licenced pub was opened and grog was available day and night: 'its effects on the poor blacks are not to be measured by words . . . the scenes enacted daily there are of a fearful character', wrote Rev. Spieseke. The pub was not ten miles from Ebenezer and the Aborigines who stayed around the pub were contacted by Nathaniel and his young friends from the mission, who encouraged them to go with them to Ebenezer.

Nathaniel's conversion was deep and powerful and he continued his work amongst the Wotjoballuk, many of whom were dying almost daily, those at the mission as well as those living on the squatters' stations. He was himself seriously ill for some time.

Then Rev. Hagenauer and his wife had to leave Ebenezer and go to Gippsland to establish another mission; this decision was made just two years after Nathaniel's baptism. During that time they had all become very fond of each other, forming a friendship that only death would break. Nathaniel was very unhappy when the couple left.

Rev. Hagenauer wrote: 'When we left Ebenezer for Gippsland in January 1862, our friend Nathaniel Pepper accompanied us about forty miles and the separation between us was a great trial to all parties. Never had I felt parting moments so deeply as when I saw our black brother disappearing in the bush near Horsham on his way back to Ebenezer.'

During the following winter, Nathaniel was taken to Melbourne where he met the Governor and was introduced as 'an Aboriginal Christian'. His cough had never really cleared up since his last illness and the week in cold Melbourne increased his discomfort. On Nathaniel's return to Ebenezer a doctor was consulted; like all his relations, he had contracted consumption.

This time he could find no relief from the pain and as Rev. Spieseke wrote, 'he allowed himself to be seduced to seek the aid of a sorcerer'. Nathaniel had sinned in the eyes of the missionary who was disappointed in the young tribesman's lack of faith and he himself was sorry that he had been to the tribal doctor. Later in the same month his brother Light died and again Nathaniel was desperately sick. His depression over Light's death made his own recovery much slower.

When he was well enough he went out from Ebenezer, visiting the surround-

---

* Depots for clothing and food were set aside and supervised by white men who were selected by the Central Board for the Protection of Aborigines. They were called Honorary Guardians.

ing stations where many of his people were living or working. He preached to them in the tribal language and taught some to read English. He also conducted services in the church of a neighbouring town.

It was said Nathaniel was taken to England for a time and on the return trip to Victoria the ship stopped at Albany in Western Australia where he met a young Aboriginal woman. They fell in love and wished to marry.[12]

That was written in a book about Nathaniel. Well I never got told that by our people. All I know is he married a young girl from West Australia named Rachel.

Henry Camfield was the Resident Magistrate at Albany and he and his wife Anne cared for many Aboriginal children who had been orphaned through epidemics of measles and influenza. One of the girls they had when they first began this work was Rachel Warndekan. She was then seven years old.

As the girls grew old enough to leave the Camfield's parental care they were faced with the problem of their future, especially as they wanted them to marry men of their own race.

'A young educated native was introduced to Mrs. Camfield's school and being fascinated with the charms of Rachel proposed marriage and was accepted, with the understanding that she should follow him to Victoria . . .'. The young man was Nathaniel Pepper.

Rachel was eighteen and Nathaniel was twenty when they were married in May 1863. The new bride fitted well into the mission life and the Moravians could see in her an aid and support for the Aborigines. She taught them reading and singing and, when Mrs Spieseke was ill, Rachel took over the school altogether.

The following twelve months were trying ones for the Peppers. Nathaniel was ill again and their first baby, a boy, died. Rachel wrote to Anne Camfield to tell her the sad news: 'we have lost our dear little baby, he was the pet of everyone here'. She told Anne how sick Nathaniel was with the pains in his chest. One day 'when he was outside he suddenly threw up some blood and he coughed and coughed'.

The missionary wrote that Nathaniel was dying and everyone was praying for him. A doctor told Rachel he could not live another month, his left lung was now completely gone. It seemed to them that the continuation of prayers resulted in Nathaniel's recovery. Once again Nathaniel returned to his evangelical work, accompanied and assisted by Rachel. Often his brother Phillip and his wife travelled with them to the camps of their people.

Then it was Rachel's turn to have days when she was unable to move far from her cottage. It was soon discovered that she had consumption. Six years after her marriage to Nathaniel, Rachel was taken to the hospital at Pleasant Creek (Stawell) where she died. Nathaniel was broken-hearted and, when his old friend Mrs Hagenauer came to Ebenezer not long after Rachel's death, he made a decision that brought unhappiness to many at the mission. He told his people he would go to Gippsland with Mrs Hagenauer.

In 1869 Nathaniel Pepper left the Wimmera, his own country, and the few surviving members of his family, forever.[13]

Nathaniel knew his brother Phillip would go on doing Christian work for the people. But then that's another story that some of Phillip's descendants might do.

Phillip carried on with his evangelical work until he died four years after Nathaniel left Ebenezer. Rebecca, his wife, died the following year.

The National Trust of Australia has an interest in Ebenezer now. 'Course the village is gone, everything is gone except the ruins of the church and a couple of cottages. Some of our people are buried in the churchyard and others are further across in the old cemetery. You can see the mounds of earth still.

My great-grandparents lie somewhere there—Nathaniel's parents Toney and Linna.

Partially restored Ebenezer buildings, 1976.

Phillip's (Nathaniel's brother) gravestone and those of the missionaries near the church ruins, 1976.

Nathaniel in Gippsland

BY THE TIME GRANDFATHER PEPPER COME TO LIVE AT RAMAHYUCK* THE bad times for the Gippsland Aborigines were over; I mean about the black hunts and all that sort of thing. This mission was on the banks of the Avon River just up from Lake Wellington. The Government let 'em have the ground, the Presbyterians helped with money and Rev. Hagenauer ran it. His wife and children lived in their own house there.

Land at Newry near Maffra was first considered as the best area for the proposed mission station but the settlers disagreed. Part of the Bushy Park station was then spoken of, but this was by-passed by Rev. Hagenauer in preference for Lake Wellington. This did not please the settlers either as they believed the land was 'too good for an Aboriginal Reserve'. Angus McMillan said the Aborigines would not live there because of the remains of their people lying at Bony Point. Legend has it many Aborigines were massacred by the whites at Bony Point. This land in the vicinity of Lake Wellington, the Perry River and the Avon River was, however, eventually made the reserve area and in June of 1863 2356 acres of land became known as the Lake Wellington Aboriginal Reserve.[1]

The new settlers seemed to be a better type of people, a lot of them were families—the first lot of settlers behaved themselves different when these others come. All the Aborigines at Ramahyuck and down at Lake Tyers where John Bulmer had his station for them at the other end of Gippsland, they had white names now. At Ramahyuck, Rev. Hagenauer used to have what he called Naming Days. All the Aborigines would stand out in the square and Rev. Hagenauer would ask if they had a name they wanted to use, a white name, and if they hadn't made up their mind about one, he'd give them the name of a settler, sometimes the man they had worked for. One lot took Rev. Chase's name, others took Rev. Kramer's, he was the missionary fella there, and of course old Billy Login had taken Rev. Login's name a long time ago. Rev. Login was a minister at Sale. A tribesman from up past Orbost got called Billy Hayes,† his name was Gobiam. Then there was a big bloke they used to say was as strong and big as a bull and he was called Billy the Bull, then William Bull. He'd fight anybody before the mission days. There were twins born once at Lake Tyers and John Bulmer called them Adam and Eve. Eve died and Adam had the surname of Cooper. Harry Derramungi was one blackfella who hung on to his Aboriginal name.

---

* The mission was first named Ramah, from the First Book of Kings: 'Samuel returned to Ramatha; for there was his house'. The Aborigines added 'yak', from *yaktun* which meant men or people belonging to the west.

† See page 99.

Aborigines in their mia-mia near Lake Wellington.

Young Braggin Scott, 1894 (The La Trobe Collection, State Library of Victoria).

The names were funny things about the Aborigines and very important to them. We never found out Grandfather Pepper's tribal name. They reckoned the Aborigines had to learn now to live the white way and that meant to start with a white name. There was another fella the old people told us about. When he was young he was a great bragger—he could do anything and knew everything—and they called him Braggin. That stuck to him all his life, Braggin Scott.

Don't you worry though, those fellas knew their tribal names in the early days when Hagenauer and Bulmer come to the missions and brought the people in. They kept their tribal names amongst themselves, 'cos we used to go up to listen to the old blokes when we was kids and they used their names to each other. We used to laugh about them, how funny they were. They wouldn't be their real tribal name 'cos they never told that—it was a secret.

When Nathaniel got to Ramahyuck there was something like one hundred Aborigines coming and goin' on the station. Some were living in little cottages they made for themselves and had a bit of a garden. Others lived in mia-mias. Rev. Hagenauer had showed them how to plant spuds and things. He had hops growing, he got well known for his hops. The place was a real little farm with the Aborigines working it to support themselves.

Grandfather must have been pleased to see Donald Cameron there; he knew him from the Wimmera. Donald married Bessy, a girl brought up in West Australia with Rachel. Another one brought to Ramahyuck from the same place was Nora and she married Charlie Foster.* They all lived at Ramahyuck.

* See page 69.

Ramahyuck School and residents of the mission (The La Trobe Collection, State Library of Victoria).

It wasn't long before Nathaniel married a Christian girl living at the station. Her name was Louise Arbuckle. They got their garden going with vegetables and he had hops too that he sold for extra money. They were happy at Ramahyuck doing a bit of fishing in the lake or river, swan-egging and possum hunting. Nathaniel helped teaching the little kids and he did his preaching too, just like at Ebenezer. He preached in the white churches sometimes.

Nathaniel Pepper was highly regarded in both the Aboriginal and white communities. In R. Brough Smyth's The Aborigines of Victoria* *he is described as 5'6½, 128 lbs and 'generally regarded as highly intelligent'. His wife Louise was said to be nineteen years old in that year of 1870 and Nathaniel would have been twenty-eight years old.*

NATHANIEL'S SECOND MARRIAGE, IS FRUITFUL

Nathaniel and Louise's children Phillip, Sammy, Percy and Lena, went to school at Ramahyuck and Rev. Hagenauer and other white neighbours had theirs there too. Bessy Cameron and Donald had the boarding house for the little kids who were orphans and she looked after them and taught in the school until they sent Rev. Kramer from Ebenezer.

Rev. Kramer had been the teacher at Ramahyuck for eighteen months when, in October 1872, the School Inspector Charles Tropp wrote in the Inspector's Register Book, 'This school has again passed an excellent examination. This is the first case since the present result system has been in force that 100 per cent of marks has been gained by any school in the colony. The children moreover show not only accuracy in their work but also exhibit much

* Page 10; Nathaniel Pepper's portrait appears on page 9.

21

BARK CANOES

Stages in the construction of a tied-ended bark canoe, photographs and notes by A. L. West,
National Museum of Victoria, 1968

At Lake Tyers, Albert 'Choppy' Hayes and Foster Moffatt prise off the bark sheet from the stringy-bark tree, a species of eucalypt.

The sheet of bark lying outer surface up on logs is trimmed down to the inner, sappy bark (both ends) to facilitate the crimping of the bark when the sheet is turned inside out.

The bark sheet is then heated to make it pliable.

The two men turn the sheet of heated bark inside out, then tie the bark with strands of stringy-bark to maintain the shape. A sharpened greenstick is used as a punch along the upper sides of the canoe wall.

Thwarts are inserted in the holes to prevent the sides of the bark from collapsing inwards.

After stiff clay from the lake margin has been used to plug cracks in the bow and stern, the canoe is launched

Ramahyuck Common School. No. 1088.

Date of Inspection	No.	NAME	Age	Standard to which each should have attained	Reading	Writing	Arithmetic	Grammar	Geography	REMARKS. Abstract of Inspector's Report on INSTRUCTION, DISCIPLINE, and BUILDING. NOTICE.—Extract from Circular 61/12, dated 9th June 1864. "The entries in the Inspector's Register are to be considered as constituting the notice, classification and report referred to in Rule 26."
	22.	Johannes Hagenauer	5, 4.							
	23.	Ida Nyary	5, 6.		3 pence each = 24					
		First Class (Highest Div.)								
	18.	Alice Pearson	7, 8.		✓	✓	✓	✓	✓	✓ 6
	19.	Emily Disher	7, 4.		✓	✓	✓	✓	✓	✓ 6
		Second Class.								
	15.	Alexander Barton	10, 6.		✓	✓	✓	✓	✓	5
	16.	Mary Ellen Darby	7, 10.		✓	✓	✓	✓	✓	✓ 6
	17.	Ida Hagenauer	7, 6.		✓	✓	✓	✓	✓	✓ 6
		Third Class.								
	10.	William Pearson	10, 0.		✓	✓	✓	✓	✓	7

Page from School Register (John Hahn of Maffra).

intelligence. *Excellent progress is shown. The discipline is very good. The children show creditable proficiency in drill and extension exercises. The deficiencies in apparatus noted at last inspection have been supplied. The School Records are carefully kept.*' Six months later Inspector Tropp was again at Ramahyuck and reported that twenty one children were present and '*the furniture and apparatus are good and sufficient. The organization is appropriate; the time-table is suitable and is strictly observed. The instruction is excellent; since my last visit a fifth class has been formed and most of the children have advanced a class.*' Bessy Cameron's brother Harry, aged fifteen, had passed the '*Standard of Education*'.[2]

The men went out of Ramahyuck to Bairnsdale to pick hops for extra money and when there was a shortage of meat for their families they were allowed to go off hunting. They were great tree-climbers and I know a few trees about there where they made the toe-holds to go up after possums and monkey bears (koala), and when they took a canoe from the big trees, they made the toe-holds first—white stringy-barks were used for canoes because the yellow splits. Well, the old Aborigine would split some bark from a sapling and tie it round the tree and then to the back of himself, fastening it with more bark. He used that to support him while he worked on the tree with his tomahawk, and when he was ready to move up the tree into another toe-hold he just leaned forward and moved the supporting bark sling up the tree.

When the bark is off the tree for the canoe it's put down on the ground and fired—the heat softens the bark, the smoke pours through it like a chimney. Then the bark is put inside-out over a big log and hit with a tomahawk to get it soft enough to pull into shape. One end is curved in and fastened with

TREE-CLIMBING

MAKING BARK CANOES

23

bark, and a sapling poked in the nose with soft bark to plug it. They'd fix in a couple of ribs and there it was, ready for fishing . . . I was talking to the Hoffmans about those big old canoe trees and some of them must be three or four hundred years old. All round where Ramahyuck was are canoe trees and possum trees. Mrs Hoffman is old Rev. Bulmer's grand daughter, and her father and mine used to go bark-stripping together in the bush.

You can see how and where the old people hunted for their food on Ramahyuck ground, where they went swan-egging and collecting grass for their bags too.

Some of the men at the mission helped Rev. Hagenauer to build the church and they put up the fence and painted it too. There's a picture of Granny Pepper standing outside that church. She told us about the bell on the church; they rang it when it was time to go to service, and everyone took notice of it. Those Aborigines were great singers and Rev. Hagenauer taught them all the songs. They reckon he changed some of them from German to English. He would give them a talk in church about Christian living and he was very down on them using any swear words. One time he lectured them about that because he heard one of the men swearing. It's a joke the old people talked about. It was when Harry Steven and Nathaniel were diggin' spuds and old Hagenauer was walkin' around and he heard Harry say to Nathaniel, 'Pass that bloody spade 'ere.' Rev. Hagenauer told the people about this in church and he said, 'I looked at that spade and there wasn't no blood on it.'

Another story the old people told us was that one day Nathaniel was in Stratford and he saw a tin in one of the shop windows with a label stuck on it. He read it and when he went back to the mission he told old Hagenauer he was very proud that day and, when Hagenauer asked why, he said, 'Because that tin had Black Pepper' written on it'.* 'Course that was his little joke.

LIVING AT RAMAHYUCK

Nathaniel married Louise Arbuckle in 1870 and they lived happily together in their cottage on the mission. When Nathaniel first arrived there, most of the people were living in mia-mias, preferring these to the restriction of a cottage. Four years later, thirteen families lived in two-roomed cottages erected by themselves.[3]

* This story was also told to the researcher by Rev. F. Hagenauer's grand daughter, Miss Hagenauer of Box Hill, Victoria.

Ramahyuck Aboriginal Mission Station, approximately 1869.

'Outwardly, Ramahyuck is a pretty settlement of white-painted weather-board buildings arranged so as to form the three sides of a quadrangle. As one approaches through the paddock from the highroad, a neat white paling fence guards the entrance to the reserve . . . at the head is the long low verandah house of the missionary superintendent with its offices and store rooms. To the right is the residence of Mr. Beilby, the State School teacher. To the left, the first building is the church with its machicolated wooden tower. Next to it is the State School. Between that and the missionary's home is a boarding house for the children. In the rear a hop kiln. In front of the compound, an extension of the sides of the quadrangle outside the palings, are the cottages of the aboriginals, all neat and nicely painted and with verandahs in front and gardens at the back. They are a far superior class to the ordinary settlers' homes . . . the neatness in the family residences, which are supplied with such evidences of civilization as stoves, water tanks, meal safes and sewing machines bought out of the earnings of the husbands and the fathers at shearing and other work . . .'

So wrote the 'Vagabond' in The Argus *of January 1886. By Nathaniel Pepper's time the village had taken shape. It was laid out on top of the hill overlooking the Avon and a large morass of green reeds, with the silvery sheet of Lake Wellington in the distance. The villagers could see the vessels on the Avon bringing visitors or groceries, clothes and the mail to the station. The township formed three sides of a very large square, the fourth side was the road from Stratford and the cottages faced into the square. Some of the Aborigines had tastefully decorated their verandas with wickerwork. Each resident had about one acre of garden for fruit trees and vegetables. Nathaniel grew his own tous-les-mois plants for arrowroot, keeping some for his family and selling the rest. Rev. Hagenauer expected the industry to become a support for all the people and had, with the help of the men, already successfully grown the plant. He had exhibited their product in Vienna, winning a medal of merit.*

Other families followed Nathaniel's lead and grew patches of arrowroot in their own gardens and were able to support themselves from the sales.[4]

In those days the banks of the Gippsland Lakes were thickly timbered and fish of all kinds plus swans and ducks gave variety to the Aborigines' diet, which included a supply of meat and milk as the farm at Ramahyuck progressed to become a self-supporting concern. The advance towards self-sufficiency was interrupted occasionally by flood, fire and lack of funds; the men were permitted to work outside Ramahyuck during these times.

Work varied on the station. At one time Nathaniel was splitting slabs six hours a day for ten shillings a week and, at the same time, keeping up with his own work in his garden. In the hop season, although he was a consumptive, he worked seven hours a day for a small weekly wage. He helped to fence the station hop garden and when it was finished the Aborigines were very proud of their work. Rev. Hagenauer said this was very important to him; that the men should be so contented with the work and the new life-style on the station.

Nathaniel often worked as a carpenter and with his friends put up a new fence at the front of the church. A visitor commented that this would improve the appearance of the village. All the school furniture was made by

Ramahyuck people gathering hops, 1877 (The La Trobe Collection, State Library of Victoria).

the Aborigines under Rev. Hagenauer's instructions, from Queensland pine. The buildings at Ramahyuck were all erected by the men, including—under one roof—a cattle-yard, the pig-sties, fowl-house and the cart-shed.

The weather was different to what Nathaniel was used to in the Wimmera and he was often sick and Rev. Hagenauer had to get the doctor to him. When he would get a bit better again he was out in the garden or on the farm working. He tried to keep up with the work and Granny Pepper helped him with their house garden. Everybody said all the people loved Nathaniel. They went to him when they were in trouble or sick or needed help; he was a real good man. Anyway he lived nearly eight years at Ramahyuck. When he died everybody was very sad, and they reckoned the white people that knew him were sad too. Nathaniel was the only Aborigine who had a headstone on his grave. All the other people had wood crosses with their names on them, but they're all gone now. Nathaniel's stone is still over the place where he was buried.

THE PASSING OF NATHANIEL
Nathaniel died at Ramahyuck thirteen years after the doctor at Ebenezer had declared that he could not live another month. He remained a consumptive, becoming weaker as the years moved on, and by March 1877 he could no

26

Ramahyuck church and school. Pupils in the care of Mrs Hagenauer on the right and her son Johannes, centre (The La Trobe Collection, State Library of Victoria).

longer walk about and was in a great deal of pain. He lay in his cottage for the last six days of his life, cared for by Louise. The Pepper home was rarely without a visitor.

Just a few days before his death Nathaniel told Louise and his friends he knew this was his last illness. He was at peace with God and felt no bitterness about his approaching death. The Aborigines in the settlement were so concerned for their friend that they took up a collection to pay for another visit from the doctor, hoping he might ease the pain for Nathaniel. When the doctor examined him, he told Nathaniel he could only hope to live at the most twelve more hours. Nathaniel was quite happy and thanked the doctor for the good news that in a few hours he would be in heaven. He was not worried about Louise and the children, he said, as they were in the safe hands of God and in the care of the missionaries. He spoke for hours with Mrs Hagenauer about the graces he had received and asked her to thank the men who had been his spiritual advisors and teachers when he was a young man at Ebenezer. Rev. Hagenauer said, 'Over and over again he declared his gratitude to us and wished us the blessings of the Lord.'

Nathaniel told Rev. Hagenauer he wanted to speak to all the people, and during his last night every person living on the station came to his bedside.

Those who were already Christians he encouraged to remain faithful to the Lord; his other friends he urged to find God so they too might be saved. Nathaniel asked them all not to leave the station where the means of grace were so freely offered to them. These words from the lips of the dying man made a great impression on them all.

Towards the morning, when his strength began to fail very fast, he asked the people to leave, 'that he might be alone with his Lord—asking that only his wife and children, my wife and myself and a few intimate friends should remain with him', Rev. Hagenauer wrote.

Louise spoke softly to Nathaniel, telling him she had forgiven someone who had sinned against her mother and who had as a result been her enemy. Nathaniel seemed very pleased. When the bell rang for morning prayer in the church, he said that it was the last time he would hear the blessed sound on earth. When Rev. Hagenauer finished the service he returned to Nathaniel's side to pray. According to the missionary, 'He then said for the last time, good-bye to us and that he would soon meet us in heaven. He thanked us again for every kindness and said, "God bless you and your children." He placed his hand in the hands of my wife and myself in farewell. Nathaniel kissed his children and gave them God's blessing in a weak voice, then he kissed his wife and while holding her hand his breath began to fail . . . as I placed my hand on his head in blessing, his soul was swiftly borne into the arms of the Saviour.' He died on 7 March 1877.

Church service at Ramahyuck, 1870 (The La Trobe Collection, State Library of Victoria).

Rev. Hagenauer said, 'We placed the earthly remains of the blessed Nathaniel into the bosom of the earth on March 8th. 1877. The whole congregation took part in the funeral service . . .'

Rev. Hagenauer had a booklet printed about his friend to give encouragement to his fellow-missionaries so, throughout the missions of the world, the story was told of Nathaniel Pepper, the first tribal Aboriginal to be baptised in Victoria. Rev. Hagenauer wrote that it had been a great privilege to attend Nathaniel during his illness and that Nathaniel and his brother Phillip when young had lived a full tribal life and, as sons of an old chief, they had a great influence over their countrymen. Nathaniel had worked as a true and faithful evangelist, conducting religious services and prayer-meetings continually among his people.

He was endowed with many noble qualities which made him beloved among the blacks as well as the whites. His kindness to everyone, his sympathy for the afflicted, his readiness to help at all times and his charity far beyond his means, were appreciated by all. As a member of the church he was always found at his place at service and his earnest prayers on many occasions in the church and elsewhere, and also within his family, were often a great blessing to many. With his good Christian wife he kept his house and garden in very good order and was able to support his wife and children, although for many years he was suffering from consumption.

After Nathaniel's death, Louise and the children moved into the mission house for a time with the Hagenauer family.[5]

Louise told Nathaniel she had forgiven the man who wronged her mother—that's what she meant. That's how the colour changed. The old people told us the Aborigines were fired on and the young white fellas took the girls and that's what happened to the mother of Louise, and she come of that—it was no fault of her mother's. Granny Pepper felt very strong about that but in the finish she told Nathaniel she forgave the white man. When the big hunts were on for the Aborigines around Yarram and the swamps, that's when Granny lost her mother. Granny got some pellets in her too and when she died a lot of years later, she still had them in her.

The Act and its Effect

THE ABORIGINES WERE DYING OUT ALL OVER VICTORIA IN THE 1880S AND the government thought they could close down the other missions they had because there weren't enough Aborigines left. They shifted our people from the Western District stations at Lake Condah and Framlingham and from the station at Coranderrk at Healesville, to the Gippsland stations. There was an Aboriginal Act* y'know and all sorts of rules there was for the people. When they lived on the stations they got a food ration and a supply of clothes and blankets. They had to sign a big book when they collected their clothes.

MIXED BLOODS EXILED FROM THE MISSIONS

As well as trying to close some of the stations and shift the Aborigines round, the government brought in a new law about sending what they called 'half-castes' off the missions and government stations, or reserves you can call them. They said anyone with white blood had to go out and fend for themselves, get jobs and houses. Sometimes if a mother was a full-blood and her husband a 'half-caste' and they had children, well then they all went out so they wouldn't be separated. When boys and girls with mixed blood reached fourteen, out they went to work for settlers as servants and farm hands. Only full-bloods could stay . . . it broke a lot of people's hearts that rule did.

A Protectorate for the Aborigines was formed in 1838 consisting of a Chief Protector and four assistants. This was terminated in 1850, but William Thomas, an Assistant Protector, continued to act as the Guardian of Aborigines. An inquiry by a select committee appointed by the Victorian Government in 1858 resulted in the formation of the Central Board for the Protection of Aborigines in 1860.†

In 1869 the Aborigines Protection Act gave the Board the authority to define 'an Aboriginal' and all those part-Aboriginal persons who were living or associating with the full-blood Aborigines were accepted as Aboriginal. Regulations imposed under this Act gave the Board extensive power in relation to these families, for example child custody, marriage, contracts. As the years passed, the mortality rates among Aborigines increased and costs of maintaining the stations rose so it was agreed by the Board to merge the remaining part-Aborigines with the white community and this meant an amendment to the Act.

In 1884 the Superintendent at Lake Condah, who had a number of Aborigines in his care, urged the Protection Board to leave the married 'half-castes' on the reserves but to waste no time in getting the Act amended so that it would be possible to send out the young 'half-castes' growing up on the reserves to

* The Aborigines Protection Act 1886.
† This lasted from 1860–1957. In 1958 the Central Board became the Aborigines Welfare Board.

Distribution of Clothing Issued to Aborigines at Ramahyuck during the Month of May & June 188

From the Clothing Books of Aboriginal Stations—Lake Wellington, 1887 (Australian Archives, Melbourne).

be apprenticed to the settlers as soon as they reached the school leaving age. By doing so, the mixed-blood on the stations would get less yearly and 'as the blacks will ere long die out . . . the whole question would be solved'. As the married 'half-castes' had the same ailments as 'the blacks' he believed 'they would not last much longer than the full blacks . . .'

In order to carry out the policy of merging the 'half-castes' with the white community, as well as those full-blood people healthy enough to leave the reserves, a detailed scheme was submitted to the Board by members of the Protection Board. The merging policy would lower the running costs of the missions and stations.

The Aborigines Protection Act 1886 reversed the definition of 'Aboriginal' and, after a short time, those people who were part-Aboriginal became officially white. Under the regulations, they were not allowed on the reserves —not permitted to stay in the cottages they had built or to live in the villages many had grown up in, nor were they entitled to camp in the paddocks once reserved for their use even with the consent of white officialdom.

The Board decided to enforce the merging of the Aborigines with the white population in such a way that all part-Aborigines under the age of thirty-four were prohibited from lands reserved for the use of Aborigines. Copies of the Act were posted up in the missions and government stations 'so those under 34 and not pure black, may thoroughly understand the position'. The people were given three years grace to find work and accommodation. Then the secretary of the Board found a flaw in the Act. He found that once off the reserves there was nothing in the Act 'to prevent the half-castes from going on to them. An order in Council might prevent it by prescribing the residence of each—but that would be difficult.' This difficulty was, however, overcome.

The Board concluded that marriages between part-Aborigines and full-bloods should be discouraged. 'The Board will use its utmost endeavours to prevent inter-marrying between Blacks and Halfcastes . . .'

By 1888 the applications received by the Board from the white settlers for boys and girls to work for them as servants were so numerous, the secretary declared, that the demand had been greater than the supply. To one applicant he explained he did not have a girl for him but asked would a young married couple suit just as well. They would take their small baby with them. If this was agreed upon, the wages would be 12s weekly for the first month, then 15s.

The members of the Board were aware that cases of hardship would arise when all part-Aborigines under thirty-four years of age were compelled to leave the reserves in January 1890 and said each case would be dealt with on its merits. The secretary wrote to the Ministry for Lands saying he thought, as the 'half-castes' were turned off the stations by an Act of Parliament, facilities should be given to them in preference to white men, in obtaining land.[1]

GRANNY PEPPER MARRIES JOHN CONOLLY

Granny Pepper's life at Ramahyuck changed about this time because she married a bloke named John Conolly. He was from Warrnambool and had been brought from one of the reserves there to work at Ramahyuck. Some time after they were married, Rev. Hagenauer thought Percy Pepper, my father, should go out and learn a trade. He was the right age, see? The new

Believed to be the first of the Conolly clan—John. The photo was taken in 1865, 'Conelly of the Goulbourn' (National Museum, Victoria).

law business. Some of the boys were already out learning farming, building or shoe-makin'. The Dad learnt baking. Those youngsters that went to school together and grew up on the mission, they stayed friends for life, helping each other and sharing what they got. It made no difference to them if the government said they were 'half-castes' or full-bloods—they were themselves, Aborigines, that's all that counted. All the tribes were mixed up when they got taken to the station; didn't matter after a while, they sorted themselves out.

Granny Pepper was now o'course Granny Conolly, and she and John Conolly had four children. When they had to leave their home at Ramahyuck because of the Act—they always called it 'under the Act'—the family lived across the road from the blacksmith's shop at Stratford and John worked there doing odd jobs like polishing leather and shoeing, all that. The blokes would say 'Hey Jack, do this for us will you?' and he kept a bit of money comin' in for tukka that way. Granny was a midwife; she used to do a lot of that around Stratford, s'pose she did at Ramahyuck too.* Their house was pulled down a long time ago but the old blacksmith joint is still there and where the saleyards were there's a bowling green now.

When we were kids we went to Granny's for holidays and she told us a lot of different stories. One time her and another young girl got stolen from their tribe's camp at Port Albert by a tribesman from the lakes. He kept them girls at his camp all night and in the morning he sent them for water but they didn't get it. They jumped in the river and swam over and linked up with the white kangaroo. See the old peoples' thinkin' belief was that if they wanted to get back to their tribe the white kangaroo took them. So the two girls followed while he hopped along, and that night they slept in a hollow log while he kept guard. He woke them in the morning by scratchin' their backs. That white kangaroo took them right back to their tribe. Their parents went to the *bugheen*, that's the clever bloke of the tribe, and got him to sing the one who took the girls away. All the men hit the sticks together and you'd hear a tic, tic, tic, and they'd sing in their language. They sang this bloke right to the camp. Well, this lakes tribesman told the elders he wanted one of these girls, so in tribal way he 'ad to prove that he could protect 'er and feed 'er. The Port Albert men stood in two lines with their spears and clubs and the lakes bloke was given a three-point shield and he had to walk up between the tribesmen while they threw the spears at 'im. If he blocked 'em that showed he was a good fighter and could protect the girl. An emu led him to the line of Aborigines and that man had to walk up the centre and protect himself with the shield. After he done that he had to prove he could feed her, so they sent him away to bring back certain parts of a kangaroo, some fish and a possum. When he did this he was allowed to have the girl. I can't remember who Granny said she was.

Those old tribal people had discipline too. They'd knock you with a waddy if you gave 'em a back answer; that learned you to do as you was told. If you was asked a question you had to tell the truth, no lies—the young people always listened to the elders. They were pretty tough on the young ones y'know. If a child wouldn't stop crying or if he'd been bad, they'd put a whole lot of leaves on the camp-fire and get it smokin', then they'd hold him over it.

* Granny Conolly's midwifery services were probably in great demand as she could speak four of the Kurnai languages fluently. Her granddaughter, Mrs Alice Young of Melbourne, states that Louise Conolly wrote the old language in a book which, many years later, was lent to an interested white man, but it was not returned. Efforts are being made to trace and recover the book.

TRIBAL LIFE: A WATER HOLE
NEAR SEASPRAY

A MASSACRE OF PORT ALBERT
TRIBESMEN

PERCY PEPPER SENT TO LAKE
BOGA AS BAKER

After that punishment they'd let him go. If you was older and you tried to cheek 'em, they'd smoke you . . . I been smoked meself . . . by old Granny Conolly.

She was always talkin' about a big water-hole near one of their camps. I saw it just the other day when I went to see a white bloke near Seaspray; he didn't want Aboriginal sites mucked up with this here pipeline that's goin' in. Now there's a story Granny told us about that water-hole. A long time ago there was a big frog lived at the hole and some of the Aborigines got that frog real wild with them, so he paid them back and drank up all the water. The tribesmen got the clever bloke again, *bugheen*, and went to the empty hole with the people. Anyway, he picked up a red-hot firestick, and he stuck it in the mouth of one of the tribesmen and he said to 'im, 'You fly away as a black cockatoo' and off the blackfella flew, a black cockatoo. See *bugheen* was tryin' to make the frog laugh, so he'd spill out the water he drunk. That didn't work, the old frog just sat watchin' all this, so the *bugheen* got some white ash on the end of the firestick and he put it on another Aborigine's mouth and he said to him, 'You fly away like a white cockatoo' and away he flew. The big frog laughed and laughed, thinkin' that was so funny, he just bursted his stomach and all the water come out his mouth and stomach and filled the hole . . . The day I was there the water-hole was dry.

It was around that area in the early days a lot of our people were massacred. Granny told us they used fire to get the Aborigines out of the bush. That young fella we talked to didn't know the right way the stories went. See, some drunk white blokes in the time when Granny was young just up and killed off a group of Port Albert tribesmen, and they paid back by killing a young white man. Then the white men all got together and hunted down a whole load of my Granny's people. This is true, y'know, but it ain't the fault of people livin' now. It's part of our history and should be told. Just the same, the story should be told right.

Aboriginal Protector George Robinson said there had been 'mischief done to the natives by some lawless and depraved white men'. They were a friendly group of Bratowoloong near the Port and they were killed by the white men who, Robinson said, were drunk.[2]

It was one of those times when Granny got to be with Arbuckle, the white man—Doctor Arbuckle. I don't know what she was, a servant, or if he looked after her or what, but that's how she got that name she said. One night she nicked off and went to a camp near Lake Wellington called Bony Point, and when Hagenauer mustered the blacks all up to Ramahyuck she went too, and that's how she come to be there when Nathaniel got to the station.

Rev. Hagenauer saved the people in them days; 'course he stopped all the tribal business on the mission. He got them to bring all their weapons and things and put 'em in a heap and burnt them. Once they was Christians there was no more of the c'roborees either.

Now after Percy, me Dad, finished that apprenticeship, he was sent up to Lake Boga near Swan Hill as a baker at a store. There was a few Aborigines livin' about there then, but before the gold days there were hundreds around Lake Boga; the Aborigines went to this store where the Dad worked for their sugar and tobacco. Some of them were his relations, descended from old Linna and Toney. Nellie Pepper, Archie Pepper's daughter, remembered when the Dad used to visit them at their house.

One of the first Aborigines to get his own land was Jackson Stewart and they had quite a little settlement of their own at Fish Point, because other people sent out of the reserves joined up with them and worked. They got their supplies from the Lake Boga store and if there was any cases of hardship amongst them that got reported to the Aboriginal Board, they sent them blankets sometimes, to pick up from the store. Young Nellie Pepper married one of the Stewarts* from the Fish Point settlement lot.

One of Dad's mates, young Johnny Ellis, turned up at Lake Boga. He was another lad who had to leave home at Ramahyuck and get work outside because he was one of our dark people who had a bit of white blood, and if those people went on to the Victorian reserves they were smartly told they was trespassing and had to get off, even if that place had been their own home since they were born.

Johnny Ellis had been working on the reserve at Cumeroogunga, New South Wales, near the Murray River. He wished to return to Victoria and wrote to the Protection Board for permission to go to the Lake Condah Aboriginal Reserve. Johnny waited for a reply from the Board to reach him at Lake Boga. His request was refused and he was told he should have remained at Cumeroogunga. The secretary of the Board advised Johnny to go to the Point McLean station in South Australia, where he would be allowed to reside. At this time Johnny Ellis and other members of his family, already had consumption.[3]

* See page 116 for Nellie Stewart's story.

amahyuck Square. Two of the Edwards children, the last family to leave the mission (The La Trobe Collection, State
brary of Victoria).

When Johnny saw Dad at Lake Boga, he gave him all the *lare-wnge*—that's our language for news—about what was goin' on at home in Gippsland. Dad's little sister Lena, who had been sent to Melbourne as a servant when she was fourteen, had gone home again to Ramahyuck where her mother, Granny Conolly and Granpa Jack Conolly were working under certificate for a while. They had to have that certificate of permission—one of the rules. Lena wasn't allowed to live with them so she stayed in Bairnsdale. Dad's brother Phillip was working outside and, when Dad saw Johnny that time, Phillip had just married Tina (Christina) McCreedie. Well I suppose with all this *lare-wnge* and the talk of the old people and home, the Dad got wantin' to go back, so he decided to clear off. Archie Pepper said he'd help him get away. Well Johnny Ellis got a couple of horses hired and Archie Pepper told Dad to 'set your bread first', and he did and then he bolted with Johnny. They left the horses a few miles out of Boga safe with some friends who took 'em back to the bloke Johnny hired them from, and they set off walking for Melbourne. From there they got a train as far as they could and then walked to Stratford where Dad got a job in the baker's near the railway crossing. They didn't have much money to get too far in the trains in those days. Later on, the Dad, Percy Pepper, married Lucy Thorpe, Billy's daughter.

The Board for the Protection of the Aborigines was informed the young man Percy Pepper had left his place of employment, he 'had run away from his employer'.[4]

Dad's brother Phillip didn't live very long after he was married, just a few years. He was about thirty years old when he died from consumption.

Phillip Pepper had undergone a severe operation at the Sale Hospital and was not expected to live. Rev. Hagenauer said Phillip 'desired to die at Ramahyuck and be buried there'. So Phillip was taken to Ramahyuck,* where he died in 1905, nine years after his marriage to Christina McCreedie.[5]

Sam Pepper, the other brother, was taken to a hospital in Melbourne and I don't know what happened to him. When he was at school at Ramahyuck, he used to teach the other kids and take charge of a class for Rev. Hagenauer. Their sister Lena married an Indian—there were a lot of them blokes about Gippsland then; well Lena and Charlie didn't have any children either, same as Phillip and Tina, but a white girl let Auntie Lena adopt her son and she brought him up. Charlie went back on a trip to India and died there. About ten years ago this adopted son of Lena's wanted to go overseas and he 'ad to get his own mother's maiden name—well I couldn't tell him and that's where it's all wrong. Adopted children should know their own identity. This is what life's all about.

---

* During the next three years after Phillip's death the families at Ramahyuck were transferred, against their wishes usually, to Lake Tyers and Coranderrk (Healesville) and by March 1908 only two Aboriginal families and the Hagenauer family remained. Ramahyuck closed in April and although one of the families moved to Coranderrk, the remaining family lived on the abandoned station for another year. A few months after they were compelled to leave, Rev. F. A. Hagenauer also left Ramahyuck forever. He died in November 1909 after having worked for and amongst the Aborigines of Australia, mainly the Victorians, for over half a century. He had during that time held the office of Secretary of the Board for some years and had been the General Inspector of Aborigines in Victoria.

The Last Tribal War

NOW WE GOTTA GO BACK TO THE 1850S WHEN GRANDFATHER BILLY THORPE
and my wife Ethel's father, George Thomas, were boys living with their own
tribe. We don't know what their tribal names were, but the tribe group was
called 'Brabuwooloong'. The real favourite campin' spot for 'em was at Swan
Reach—beautiful there, they had all they wanted in the way of tukka. They
went swan-eggin' and had plenty of fish, and going back across through the
bush, they had a track to Bunyarnda (a white bloke called it Lake Tyers)
where they caught monkey bears and possums, kangaroos and wombat.
Birds—everything. They called meat *nullee*, 'pass that *nullee*' they'd say. If
there was a possum in a tree the blackfellas cut toe-holds with a stone
axe—those marks are still there today—and run up the tree after the
possums. Sometimes they trimmed away the branches for a sittin' place if the
tree was near water, and the old blackfella would make noises like the ducks,
'wuk, wuk, wuk', and when the duck come round, he just threw his stick or
boomerang at it and the little kids had to get out there and pick up the dead
duck. Sometimes they were just stunned. They caught the water-hen that
way too.

Their country began at the Tambo River, right up it, then over to Buchan
and down to Tyers, Bunga, Metung, all round there, and a bit of Lake King,
and back to the Tambo. Now that was their territory and no other tribe could
come on it unless they had permission, and they couldn't cross the Tambo
neither, that belonged to the south tribe.

*Gippsland was Kurnai country. The men were of one order, Yerang, and the
women were Djeetgang; both these totems were small birds. Groups within
the whole tribe of Kurnai held their own territory and name.*

*The Bratowoloong were in South Gippsland. The Brayakoloong owned the
district around Sale through to the mountains. The people at Lake Tyers
were the Warn-a-ngatte. Eastward to the Snowy River were the
Krowathunkooloong. The Brabuwooloong held Central Gippsland. The Boul
Boul Metung lived on the island and a strip of land along the coast bounded
on the other side by the lakes and they belonged to the group Tatungolong of
the lakes, islands and coastal section. Wooloom Bellum Bellum were around
Sale and Rosedale, the district of the Brayakoloong.[1]*

Sometimes they crossed over the Tambo River, the boundary, both sides did,
to pinch women or have a payback, then there was a fight, but they were
mostly peace-lovin' people. They had their friendly meetings, corroborees,
and swapped songs and stones for axes, and sacred ceremonies they had too.
These tribal businesses got messed up when the cattle and sheep took up the

37

Lake Tyers. *(left to right)* William Johnson, Lance McDougall, Johnny McDougall, (small boy), Alec Moffatt.

hunting spots and the whites killed the kangaroos to keep 'em off the stock runs. After a while the Aborigines wasn't wanted on the runs and that's when the tribal fights got earnest 'cos they had to hunt on some other tribe's ground.

The last big tribal fight, war really, was fought at the mouth of the Tambo River between Billy Thorpe's tribe and the South Gippsland mob—the Port Alberts. It lasted all day and right into the evening. How it come about was the other tribe had got to the Tambo food-hunting and they decided to swim over for swan-egging, but word soon reached the Swan Reach Aborigines and they got together, the men and the women too, and off they went with their war weapons, barbed spears, waddies, sticks and killer boomerangs. The killer boomerang is sharp on both ends; the game boomerangs were shaped different and spun round and round and come back.

The children were left in the camp with all the old people or anyone sick, they never went to the fights. Billy and George were only young lads and after the warriors left they nicked off after 'em, following for miles without being caught. They got to part of the country where fires had been through and they had a job hiding there, just burnt trees, stumps and logs. They got spotted. Well, it was too far back to the old people, so their parents left them there, but well hidden in an old hollow log covered over with burnt branches. Grandfather told me 'it was 'olla all right but it 'ad plenty stingin' nettles inside'. Their people told these boys not to move out of that log till they got back.

The tribes met at the mouth of the Tambo River and they had a terrible battle, a lot of them killed and wounded on both sides. Grandfather told me 'it wasn't till dusk our people come back past where we was, still in that 'olla log and we was howlin' and yellin', and it was old Kitty Johnson and Dick Cooper who found us. My parents were both dead in the battle and so were George's. Kitty took us and reared us up.' Old Dick Cooper,* he was one of the real tribal ones like Kitty. They were in Gippsland when the whites first come; same as all those others in that last tribal war.

It was a few years after that† John Bulmer started the mission at Lake

* See page 97.
† 1860.

'Open Air Service' at Lake Tyers, 1870 (The La Trobe Collection, State Library of Victoria).

JOHN BULMER FOUNDS LAKE
TYERS MISSION

Tyers, but he was going to have it up near Buchan; but our people said they knew a better place where there was fresh water and native food and they took him to Bunyarnda and that's how Lake Tyers started. All the Aborigines had come for years from as far as Manaroo (Monaro) to Bunyarnda; it was a sort of meeting place. They did a lot of spear fishing there with the kangaroo bone. They had these big rocks for sharpening bone and axes on—there's some of these about Gippsland now you can see—and they'd sharpen up points on the bone, then get the sinew from a kangaroo tail and fasten the bone with it to a lump of tree neatened into a stick. Next the resin from a tree was heated and poured over the binding and they were ready for fishing. You know what they used for salt? The flower off pigface, they ate that. It grows all over the joint.

WORKING AS STOCKMEN FOR
THE SETTLERS

Most of the Aborigines who were at Lake Tyers or come there when John Bulmer did couldn't speak English; only those that had worked for settlers and they didn't settle there all at once either. Billy Thorpe and George Thomas had worked on the Orbost station as young stockmen and they told us they were given their white names by the farmers then. When they went to Bulmer they knew how to talk English, but they were only young fellas even then.

One of the young tribesmen who worked for Macleod at Orbost was named Billy Macleod by the white family. His own name was Tulaba and he was the son of a warrior and a nephew of the famous Kurnai warrior Bruthen Munji. Tulaba was sent with his own young family, to guide John Bulmer to Gippsland through the scrub, bush and gullies, in order to form the Aboriginal station. At that time John Macleod was Honorary Protector of Aborigines at Orbost and distributed food and clothing to the Kurnai who by then had no camping or hunting grounds left to them.

One time when Billy Thorpe and George went out they got mustering jobs with Stirlings up near Cape Conran. Out from there is a reef called 'Beware' and the ships had to beware. Well, one time when they came riding round one of the points at Cape Conran there was wreckage on the beach from some ship that had smashed up on the reef. They saw this big thing on the sand and jumped off the horses to take a closer look. They'd never seen anything like it

39

before and they poked at it and pushed it, then one of 'em got a stick and whacked it; it made a noise at them, so they both gave it a few cracks and when it made more noises back at them they jumped around banging into it with their tomahawks and they didn't let up till it was smashed and couldn't make no more squeaks and growls. That was the first piano they ever saw.

Further along the beach was a box, a chest, but no risks with that, they didn't try to open it, just pulled and shoved it up into the scrubby bush near a big tree, dug a great big hole and buried it. Y'know, they never went back to get that chest. Years later Grandfather Thorpe told his son Henry about the chest, then Henry told his son Reggie about it and where it was hid, but neither Grandfather Billy or George Thomas would get it. Us young ones reckoned we'd get it and we went there in our old car, but we hit a bridge and broke the axle and that was as far as we got. Reggie said to me, 'The old fellas 'ave cursed us—they never wanted us to find it.' We been back a few times over the years for picnics there and always 'ave a joke about it, but we never have found it. One of the Nixons told me I could have a loan of a tractor to dig about but—ah—I wouldn't know where to start lookin' for sure. Anyway we reckon the old people don't want us to find it for some reason.

Before the mission days a few of the young dark fellas worked on the Macleod's station at Orbost, a big one around the Snowy River. There was Joe Banks and Billy Macleod and two brothers Charley and Billy Barlow were some of them—Billy Thorpe and George Thomas too, and most of them would've been in their middle teens. The tribal people had a camp down near the coast where the Snowy comes out, *murraloo* where there was a lotta mud and morass and the water back a bit was only ankle deep. They went there in the winter for swan-egging . . . it's called Marlo now. The Milly was another camp not far off—a scrub on the Brodribb River where the creek goes into the river, nice and reedy.

When Billy and George were mustering they'd camp on the Snowy near where Orbost is now. From there they'd go down to the Milly where the blackfellas were camped and talk to them in their language.

GIN-HUNTS

See, there were a lot of queer white blokes about at that time, men working for the stations, most of 'em convicts. Some had done their time, some were working out their sentences and plenty of them were escaped convicts who come in along the Gippsland coast. They ran loose around the place. Didn't have any women of their own and they shot the tribesmen and chased the women—and they got 'em too. They never just shot at them, they slaughtered a lot of the Aborigines to get the women . . . that's where the change of the colour often come in.

Grandfather told us the white men had 'gin-hunts'—come down on their horses to get the women in the camps. If ever him or George heard the white blokes talking about a 'gin-hunt', they'd whip off and go down and warn 'em. One of the times when they heard the talk going on they took a short cut to the Milly camp to warn the blackfellas or the *koories* or Aborigines or *gunai* or whatever you want to call 'em. They knew the white men always had guns.

Well the tribe 'ad a coupla smart gins stand well back—see—and when the gin-hunters saw the women they got off their 'orses. Some of the tribesmen were hidden in the reeds and they made noises to make the white men think there were more women there than they could see. When the white fellas got far enough away from their horses, movin' in after the girls, some of the blackfellas raced out of the reeds and grabbed the guns from the horses and

40

fired on the white men. 'Course they didn't know how to hold the guns properly, some even held them upside-down, they just fell backwards into the grass . . . they only had one chance. That was one time the Aborigines got their women away safely.

As the years went by and Grandfather Thorpe got old, he told me all these things.

When the big stations were cut up for the selectors some of them let the Aborigines stay on the land because it was the place where they was born and lived, but as the monkey bears and kangaroos and all the native food got short, more of 'em settled down on the missions. Billy and George went too and learned to read and write and John Bulmer taught any of the Aborigines who wanted to listen the stories in the Bible. He understood the people and their tribal ways and, as the different tribes came together, there wasn't many of 'em left and if they had an argument to fight over he'd just say to them, 'Let's talk it over', and they all sat down and talked.

That Orbost station was owned by Sir William Clarke after Macleods left and somtimes George Thomas worked for him as a station hand. Clarke had a few dark fellas working for him, but I don't think they seen much of him, he had a white man managing for him and that one was the boss. Billy Thorpe said he worked there while Clarke had Orbost too. Mary Gilbert in Bairnsdale put out a book with stories in it from old residents of Orbost and one woman said her father was the foreman for Clarke. He was good to the Aborigines and they liked him; years after, when the station was cut up, George Thomas, Harry Derramungi and the Chases and some of the other fellas used to go and visit that foreman and he'd give them a feed and the Aborigines always left boomerangs or some baskets made by the women.

Billy and George were two of the first lads to go to the established mission station, under the twenty-seven-year-old manager, Englishman John Bulmer. He wrote:

> *'Many a poor blackfellow was ruthlessly shot down, who really was in no sort of mischief. A case occurred on the site of the present station. Before we occupied the station, it was a sheep station. A house was built near the site of our present homestead, in which lived the shepherd and the hut-*

Aborigines at Lake Tyers prior to 1909. Back row third from left is John Bulmer and Kitty Johnson is fifth (Stratford Historical Society).

The men of Lake Tyers were carpenters, brick-layers and painters. They built these cottages and furnished them. John Bulmer is with the front group, 1886.

keeper. There were a few blacks camping on one of the arms of the Lake and having caught a great many mullet, one of the old men proposed to take some to the white-fellows, so with a little boy, (who afterwards told me the story) they started, each carrying fish.

'When within sight of the hut, the boy noticed the white man signalling to them to be off. The old man took no notice, but went on with the fish.

'Soon the boy heard a gun fired and saw the old man fall, of course he did not wait. He dropped his fish and ran off to tell the tribe.

'Thus the old man lost his life in trying to do a good turn to the white man and thus the blacks were embittered and took revenge whenever they could.'

John Bulmer said some of the so-called murders of whites were only acts of revenge by the natives for injury done to them by the whites.

One tribesman told Bulmer that once when he was a boy and out hunting with his mother and father the mother was left to make the camp, as was the usual thing, while the father was hunting. 'Late that night, he crawled back to the mother and son with a gaping wound in his side, and said the white fellow shot him. Many other cases of a similar kind occurred, which shows that after all, some of the so called murders were but an act of justice.'[2]

Mr and Mrs Bulmer started teaching the Aborigines who were camped at the lake and after a while Mrs Bulmer showed some of the women how to sew dresses, different to sewing animal skins together with bone and sinew, eh?

Young Dick Cooper and Neddy O'Rourke could speak English too. Then there were other young blokes who had been brought up by white families

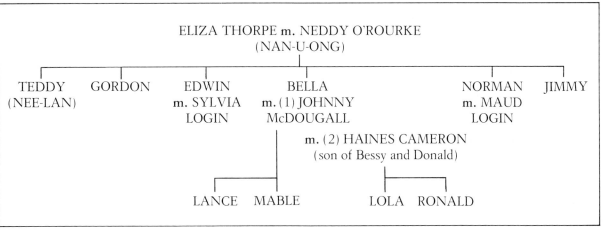

ELIZA THORPE m. NEDDY O'ROURKE
(NAN-U-ONG)

TEDDY (NEE-LAN)   GORDON   EDWIN m. SYLVIA LOGIN   BELLA m. (1) JOHNNY McDOUGALL   NORMAN m. MAUD LOGIN   JIMMY

m. (2) HAINES CAMERON
(son of Bessy and Donald)

LANCE   MABLE   LOLA   RONALD

who went to the mission, and some others were just workin' for the early white squatters and had no family life. Neddy was adopted by the white family of O'Rourkes. He was a baby when they found him and took him in. They taught him all about farmin' and when he grew up he married Billy Thorpe's sister Eliza.

Five O'Rourke brothers came to Australia during the early 1840s. Two of these young men settled in Gippsland in 1845. One of them, James, built his home at Wulgulmerang (Woologoramarang) on the Monaro road near the Snowy River in 1848.

When the massacre of Aborigines occurred at Butcher's Ridge in the north of Gippsland, James found a baby boy, believed to be the only surviving member of the group. James O'Rourke adopted the baby, giving him his own surname and the Christian name of one of his brothers, Edward.

As the boy grew older he was called Neddy. The O'Rourkes always allowed Neddy to visit his own people, the Kurnai. Neddy lived for many years with the O'Rourke family, learning to work and live in the white peoples' style.

When he was a young man, Neddy left his white family and joined John Bulmer at the mission on Lake Tyers. Bulmer said Neddy O'Rourke 'brought his character written by his old employer, O'Rourke. It was a very good one. He was praised for his faithfullness and zeal to do his Master's wish.'

Neddy O'Rourke married Eliza Thorpe, 'with whom he lived for over twenty-four years'. John Bulmer said Neddy was a very good fellow and led a good life. He died in 1902, aged fifty-eight.

Eliza told John Bulmer a story in which her own grandfather was the 'chief actor'. There was a power possessed by some men of the tribe that enabled them to take life in a secret way. The power was called kooloot. *The men of the tribe who inhabited the district of Raymond Island had killed a man of the Brabuwooloong. The Brabuwooloong lived in the land where Bairnsdale now is. 'The actors marked the shape of the man they wished to punish, on the ground, and sang their charm song, using his real name . . . he came to them from where he had been fishing. They gave him a possum to eat and told him he would die . . .' A short time later the tribesman died.*[3]

That's right. We know about that story, only I didn't know it was my old ancestor who had that power.

People of Lake Tyers. *(left to right) Back:* John Bulmer, Andrew Chase, Big Joe, Mary McRae, William Johnson, Edward McDougall, Ted Moffatt, Mrs Jennings, Mrs Ted Foster, Teddy O'Rourke, Billy Hayes, John Rivers, NEDDY O'ROURKE. *Front:* ELIZA O'ROURKE (NÉE THORPE) with son EDWIN, Catherine Chase, Ellen Hood holding Malcolm Rivers, Maggie Johnson holding Bob Johnson, Caroline Hayes holding Harry Hayes, 1895 (Nora Cochrane).

Eliza O'Rourke told us that when she was a little girl the people were down c'roborin' at Bunga Creek, bangin' their sticks and singin' and going on, when up the creek come a boat with some *lohans* rowing it, leanin' over tasting the water, lookin' for fresh water, see? That was the first time some of those blacks saw a white man, she said. 'Course they stopped c'roborin' and stood there looking at these white blokes. One *lohan* got out of the boat and come over to them and they poked him and felt him, rubbing his skin, then he got out his pipe and lit it up. The blacks jumped on him and threw him in the water to put him out Granny O'Rourke said. When this bloke puffed out the smoke the blackfellas all let out a howl. When he got out of the water he showed them the pipe and showed them a gun, too, and how it went off. The white men were friendly to the Aborigines and Granny said her people knew they wanted fresh water, so they led them to it.

Granny O'Rourke could remember when the clever fellas were about from the tribes and, if they wanted to punish anyone, they followed his track, then drive a spear into the mark of 'is foot and that blackfella would get a poisoned foot and die. Those fellas had this special power and they could *nur-ritch* a person; that means they could sit down in the bush and point the bone, or sing you. Anyone they did that to couldn't move any further and if they wanted to kidney-fat them, they could then. *Nur-ritch-bun* means take the kidney fat. They did that with a long stick with a bone hook on it and they'd get out a main nerve. 'Course the poor fella would die. Granny O'Rourke remembered when the bad spirits, *mur-raage*, were about the place too.

The tribespeople always got their fire-stick at Bunga she told us. They kept their fires going with the white fungus from the gum-tree. A big piece of this fungus was stuck on a long stick and carried around with them wherever

TRIBAL LIFE: POINTING THE BONE

TRIBAL LIFE: MAKING FIRE-STICKS

44

they went. It would burn for weeks and weeks, going from one stick to another.

Well anyway, Eliza and Neddy O'Rourke had Teddy—they always called him Nee-lan. After him they had Edwin, Bella, Jimmy, Norman and Gordon.

Then Billy Thorpe married Lily at Lake Tyers and they had about three babies that died before they had Rachel, who was a sick child, always had trouble with her eyes. Then there was Annie, Lucy (my mother), Henry and Leslie.

There were a lotta children about with no parents living at Lake Tyers. Some of these children were orphans and some were left there by their people to have the Bulmers teach them, so they built an orphan-house and Billy and Lily Thorpe lived there for a while in charge of those children.

Well Lily Thorpe and Eliza O'Rourke did a lot of sewing after Mrs Bulmer taught them and when material come from the government they sewed it up for the people. They got sent a sewing machine of their own from the government because they was so good at it.

The families were baptised at the mission and Billy was confirmed there, too; it was a Church of England mission y'know. The church is still there—St John's.* It was built by John Bulmer and the Aborigines on the station, most of it, and Grandfather use to talk about that and how John Bulmer built that pulpit himself. They built the pews too. There's a photo of a wedding when John Bulmer was a minister taken at the church with a mob of us.

Billy and Neddy put a lot of the fencin' up on the station and some of

* The Aboriginal Protection Board notes in 1873 that William Thorpe was confirmed at St John's Church on Lake Tyers.

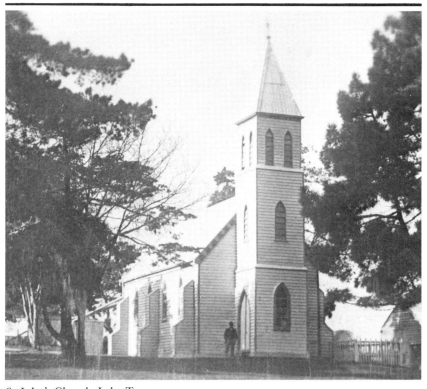

St John's Church, Lake Tyers.

Billy's is still there. They used timber off the station land and that was used for the church pulpit, benches and stools as well.

When money and food was short on the mission, John Bulmer let the men go out to work with the settlers. He let them go out hunting the old native food too, but, as the years went on and more white people took up land, animals and roots got short as well. When there wasn't any money on the mission to buy rations, John Bulmer put his own money in—I know that for a fact. He would get some beef and milk for the little kids from somewhere. The men on the mission who were not old or sick went lookin' for the work but the trouble was, there were more settlers getting about by then and the stations had them working for them, so that made it harder for the dark people to get jobs on the farms.

George Thomas married a young girl named Agnus at Lake Tyers too. They were Ethel's parents. Now when Agnus was small (about 1864) her tribespeople brought her to John Bulmer and asked 'im to look after her and bring her up 'cos they thought she had more chance on the mission than living in the scrub and bush at Delegate, that's Manaroo country. Anyway, after a few years when the first teacher John Bulmer had was leaving with his family to live away from Lake Tyers, he wanted to take Agnus with him and adopt her, but they wouldn't let that happen because John had promised her tribe he would look after their little girl who was named Agnus at the mission.

THE THOMAS FAMILY

Christmas at Lake Tyers. Kitty Johnson on the left of the table and John Bulmer on the right, 1906.

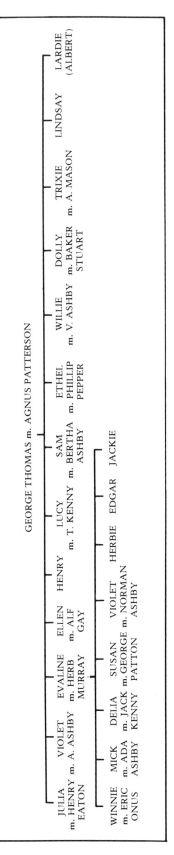

George and Agnus had Julia and Evaline at the mission station, but about that time all the people that were not called full-blood had to go out, so the Thorpe and Thomas families left the mission.* George took his family to Newmerella and they lived in a *mia-mia* for a while till they got a little cottage built. He worked snaggin' the Snowy and clearing up logs brought into it during floods. They'd dig big holes and drag the logs into them with bullocks and burn them. There was a lot of fellas clearing the Snowy flats. He did all the work he could get, mustering stock round the coast and he overlanded cattle from Albury while Agnus looked after the children.

When John Bulmer wrote the following note about George Thomas, Agnus had ten children. They eventually had fourteen children, thirteen of whom lived to adulthood, eight girls and five boys.

'George Thomas went to Orbost where he has raised a family of ten children, mostly girls, one, the eldest daughter is a trusted servant with a friend there and he informs me he does not want a better servant. She is all that can be desired; the rest of his girls are in various situations so that the father is relieved of anxiety as to their future.' [4]

* See page 32.

An Aboriginal is

THERE WAS THIS STORY THAT WAS TOLD ABOUT A WHITE BLOKE SPEARED at Orbost not far from where the Thomas's lived. It happened a long time before they went there to live.

THE STORY OF DAN, THE CONVICT, AND THE ABDUCTED TRIBAL GIRL

Dan was one of them convicts and he worked for Macleods on the Orbost station. Well, he used to go after the black girls and one day he caught one, just a young girl. He kept her for himself, locked up in his hut, tied up 'alf the time so's she couldn't get away. He had her there for three days. This Dan kept stickin' hot ashes out round the door of his hut so the blackfellas would get their feet burnt when they come lookin' to get her, and that was a silly thing to do because they just waited for the coals to get cold—and that's probably how his hut got on fire. They reckoned the Aborigines fired it. When Dan come out of the hut he had 'is gun but got no time to use it because the tribesmen were waitin' with their spears ready. They threw that many that the bloke never fell down. He was propped up with spears. The tribesmen took the girl away with them.

The Commissioner of Crown Lands in Gippsland, Charles Tyers, reported the death of the convict Dan Moylan to Superintendent La Trobe. Tyers suggested that because of 'the attack' made by the tribesmen on the Snowy River Station extra police should be ordered to Gippsland for the settlers' protection, and troopers were sent to the district. Four months later, the police at Bombala had several tribesmen in custody, 'on suspicion of being concerned with Moylan's death'.[1]

Kurnai Tribesman photographed by Antoine Fauchery in 1857 (The La Trobe Collection, State Library of Victoria).

Some white people said the Gippsland blacks of the 1850s was getting what they called civilised, and if the early squatters had tried to get to know them and their tribal rules, a lot of the Aborigines wouldn't have got killed when the chase after them got under way after the tribesmen killed Dan the convict.

'The blacks were becoming civilised and if they had been treated fairly, it is believed that the tragedy of the murder of Little Dan, the cook, would not have occurred. It was a case of retributive justice according to their tribal laws.'[2]

In the real early days our people didn't wake up about bullets. They'd just stand there and get shot. Didn't understand how they got hit with something and fell over from *lohans* pointing something at 'em. They tried to fight back with boomerangs, killer boomerangs and spear, but they found out it wasn't the same as chasing a kangaroo.

MASSACRE AT THE MILLY

Word soon got around that Dan was dead and the white men come from all over the place and made up a party and come after the Aborigines on their horses. They found them in their camp at the Milly near the Brodribb River. There were men, women and children in that camp and the whites shot a lot; we don't know how many. Some of the young lads got away but they were found and brought up on the Orbost station as stock riders and musterers and general farm hands. Those young fellas had the name given of Macleod and Banks. One of the young fellas was Harry Derramungi, and he always kept the Derramungi—never changed it to a white name.

Years ago at Orbost they had two big stones outside the butter factory as a landmark for Dan where he was buried. The white blokes were tellin' me the blackfellas murdered him and I said, 'Yer all wrong. He deserved to get killed for what he did to a young tribal girl; he kept her there in the hut and used her up.' I asked one of the blokes how would he feel if a daughter of his had been taken by the same man and tied up and treated in the same way. What would he have done?

There was all sorts of ways the white blood got into the black. I know there was sealers and whalers climbing in along the Gippsland coast before the squatters were here and that's where some of the white blood came in, and then when the first cattle and sheep men and their workers arrived, more got in. That's what made it hard on the tribal women when they had a baby and it wasn't properly dark. They thought there was something gone wrong with their husbands.

Nathaniel Pepper was one that was full-blood amongst my grandparents, but Louise had a white father. Billy had white blood in him, but his wife Lily didn't, but we don't know what tribe she was from. Billy lived along the Tambo and all around that country—I told you—him and George Thomas and Eliza, Billy's sister, all had some white blood. They was all born around the 1840s, far as we know.

Then there were shipwrecks along the coast and Granny said her people saw the boats. There was a story about women from the wrecks who was taken by the tribes and looked after and were wives to some of the tribesmen and there were supposed to be some children from that too. I asked old Granny one time if there was any truth in those stories and she said, 'It might have been true, could be true, but it mightn't be either.'

When the selectors come in, some of them got little kids from the tribes and adopted 'em. The little dark girls, they dressed 'em up like fancy dolls. They'd have a great big bow stuck on top of their heads bigger than their face sometimes and they'd be dollied up in smart clothes, socks 'n shoes and clean as a pin. Those little kids got to think they was better than their own people, the dark people, and as they got older a lot didn't want to have nothing to do with the Aborigines. Then there were others who wanted to go back to the Aborigines and often nicked off and they made the whites wild with them. Other times the white mother didn't want them any more when they got over eight or ten years old—see they were cute while they were younger—and those children were mixed up then all right. They didn't know who they belonged to, only their skin was dark. They'd been show-pieces first, then often servants to the family they were with after.

We had a couple in our family who lived with whites, but they were good white people. Mabel Kramer was taken when she was little but they let her see the dark relations from time to time so she didn't lose her identity. Neddy O'Rourke was the other. The O'Rourkes brought him up good and he was allowed to visit the Aborigines. He turned out a real good blackfella.

Yer can't tell a dark fella he is not Aborigine. He's not white, is he?

Granny Louise was dark but I'm fairer than her. Different people ask me how I come my colour. One bloke asked me at a meeting recently and I said to him, 'If you was among a lot of black girls you'd leave your strain there.'

White and black paint are two different colours. Pour 'em together and they're mixed.

Ethel's a different shade to me so our children have been darker or lighter. Our daughter married a white man and their children are white and the strain is finished. This is how it works.

I always say when I see a white person and he's brown, there's a different strain of blood there. Same in the black race. You see Aboriginal girls about Bairnsdale with white babies and children. In years to come there'll be hardly any black people.

I hear some of the *unyai*—fellas that haven't got to be a older person like me in me seventies—don't take to the Aborigines gettin' called native. Well the way I see it a native is a person who lived here in Australia all his life, an Aboriginal born here. They can't argue over that. Now you take the white man, when he come here he was only colonial, see? And today they might be Australians, but not a real one. The REAL Australian is the Aboriginal black . . . mixed, blue or brindle, what you want to call him, the descendants of the old people, the tribal people. The black people never migrated into this country, they were here, put here by our Saviour, y'see, the Lord Jesus Christ. He's the man took them to this place, He put 'em here.

The white come here and took it by force with a lotta blood bein' shed by the Aborigines, they really died for their own country and got nothin' in return.

Today that war is over between the white and black people, we're one people, our men fought in the wars together overseas.

Like Grandfather said, we have got to learn to live with each other.

Phillip and Ethel Pepper's great grandchildren: Richard, Robbie-Lee and Russell Stanton.

The Colour of Your Skin

If you believe because you're white that you're among the chosen few,
Well then you'd better think again, that's what you better do.
For you should never judge a person by the colour of their skin,
For the colour is just the outside—we're all the same within.

So whether they are yellow, white, black or red
Remember, God has made us all upon His earth to tread.
And when the roll is called up yonder, and the saints go marching in,
He won't choose His loved ones by the colour of their skin.

By Geoff Hahn[3]

CHAPTER SIX

Grandfather Billy Thorpe

SELECTION AT LAKES ENTRANCE

BILLY THORPE TOOK HIS FAMILY TO LIVE AT CUNNINGHAM, THAT'S LAKES Entrance now, and he got work with the Roadknights at Merrangbaur. They hadn't been there very long when their baby son Leslie died. Then one day in the same year, 1889, when Billy was working in the paddock someone come down to tell him Lily was crook, and he ran all the way back to the house but she was dead. She got a haemorrhage while she was coughing and the blood kept coming up. Lily was only thirty-two. Billy was left with four young children—Rachel, Annie, then seven years old, Lucy who was five, and Henry was three years old.

Well, after a while they got this woman to come and help Billy with the children and he ended up marrying her. She was Sarah Dawson from Warrnambool. They had a daughter Alice; we always called her Allie. After a while Lucy and Annie were old enough for work and Rev. Bulmer and Rev. Hagenauer got jobs for these young girls with some settlers in Melbourne for 7s a week.

Work ran out for Billy and he got employment back at Lake Tyers fencin' and the family got rations there while they lived for a while on the station. Work was so hard for the men to get that the government helped with blankets and rations. A lot of them were too sick to work anyway. Billy had bad health too. Anyway, after getting more work like strippin' bark he had enough to select a bit of ground at Lakes Entrance, ten acres belonged to him and he bought it for the survey fee of half a crown an acre. He grew beans and spuds on 'is little farm.

John Bulmer reported that: 'On the passing of the "half-caste" act, there were two men William Thorpe and George Thomas who had to leave the station to mingle with the white population. These two with their wives and children left. W. Thorpe went to the township of Cunningham where he has led a very consistent life proving by his industry that he could earn his own living. He has brought up his family respectably; indeed for his youngest daughter he has purchased a piano and had her taught music. She is able to play fairly well. He has been able to take his place among white people and has helped his district in various ways. When a schoolhouse was required he gave his pound with the rest'. John Bulmer added to his comments that because of many visits of Aborigines who were not working, Billy Thorpe's nose 'was kept to the grindstone'.[1]

PERCY MARRIES LUCY THORPE

Henry Thorpe grew up and married Julia Scott, Braggin's sister, and they had their house on the farm too. They built the house from the farm timber; it was a split palings and bark house. Then, when Lucy come home to the farm, she met Percy Pepper who was workin' around there. Percy fell for her and they got married. So there you have it.

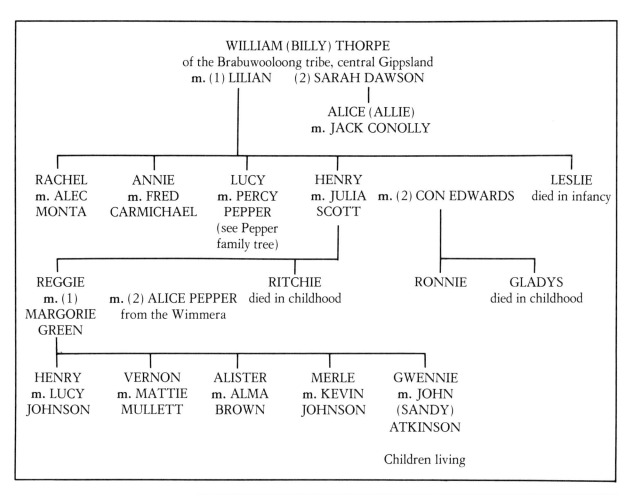

WILLIAM (BILLY) THORPE
of the Brabuwooloong tribe, central Gippsland
m. (1) LILIAN   (2) SARAH DAWSON

ALICE (ALLIE)
m. JACK CONOLLY

RACHEL
m. ALEC
MONTA

ANNIE
m. FRED
CARMICHAEL

LUCY
m. PERCY
PEPPER
(see Pepper
family tree)

HENRY
m. JULIA
SCOTT   **m.** (2) CON EDWARDS

LESLIE
died in infancy

REGGIE
m. (1)
MARGORIE
GREEN   **m.** (2) ALICE PEPPER
from the Wimmera

RITCHIE
died in childhood

RONNIE

GLADYS
died in childhood

HENRY
m. LUCY
JOHNSON

VERNON
m. MATTIE
MULLETT

ALISTER
m. ALMA
BROWN

MERLE
m. KEVIN
JOHNSON

GWENNIE
m. JOHN
(SANDY)
ATKINSON

Children living

Henry and Julia's home of bark and split palings. *(left to right)* Reggie Thorpe, Freddie Webb, Sam Pepper, Julia Thorpe, Dora Pepper, Ivy Webb. Phillip is in front of Dora and Gwen Pepper is on the extreme right, 1914.

Annie Thorpe got married to a full-blood named Fred Carmichael from
Warrnambool way. He was on the Lake Condah station, and Annie not being
a full-blood it caused a lot of trouble, because the laws were changed and they
said Annie was a white girl and couldn't live on the station with Fred and if
he wanted to live with her he had to leave the station. All I know was there
was problems. He was a cruel bloke and Annie left 'im after a few years and
went to Orbost to live.

When the mission stations broke up, Freddie lived at Lake Tyers. He
played a lot of cricket around about Sale, then he went to Melbourne to play
and he was hittin' sixes everywhere. He had a keen eye and watched the
bounce of the ball and knew when to stroke. As the ball left the bowler's hand
he could tell pretty well what pace it was goin' and when to strike. Bein' a
full-blood he had sharp eyes—all Aborigines are sharp-eyed people, that's
why they made such good trackers. Con Edwards and Chook Mullett were
another coupla good cricketers and when they was invited to Melbourne to
play with a club for a match, they sang out to each other in their own
language and none of the white fellas knew what they said.

*The missioner at Lake Condah Aboriginal Station, north-west of Port Fairy,
advised Fred Carmichael in 1900 not to marry 'this half-caste girl', Annie
Thorpe. Regulations in force were such that a part-Aboriginal person could
not receive rations on the reserve and if Fred wished to marry Annie Thorpe
he would have to leave Lake Condah and therefore lose his cottage and his
supplies. Annie was indeed considered, by law, to be a white girl.*

*Fred married Annie in May 1900 and defied authority by taking her to live in
his cottage at Lake Condah. The missioner gave Fred rations but his wife was
not permitted to receive food. This troubled the missioner so much that he
asked the Board to request the Solicitor-General to make a decision giving an
interpretation of the law regarding Annie, but the Board refused to refer the
matter further. The missioner was upset, but accepted the decision.*

Annie and Fred left their home on the station.

*After trying to make a living outside for three years, Fred, Annie and their
child returned to Lake Condah. The missioner asked the authorities to let the
Carmichael family live permanently on the station. This request too was
refused.[2]*

Grandfather and Uncle Henry dug a dam on the farm for their own fresh
water supply, and they planted apple and plum trees too. Henry had a
training track up from his house. He was a great hurdler and Dad used to
train him. They told us back in 1901 when Jack Donaldson the world
champion and Arthur Postle* come out here, Frank Moon and my father
were running together and Frank won the Lakes Entrance Gift, worth ten
pounds, a lot of money in those days, and my Dad won the seventy-five sprint
. . . Frank and Dad were out settin' rabbit traps when one time Frank found
one of the caves at Buchan, early in the 1900s.

The Dad took any work going. When I was about six, Mum and Dad went
picking maize near the mouth of the Tambo and old Mr Howlett, who owned
the land there, told Dad that when he was ploughing the paddocks along the
river he bumped into the old stone tomahawks everywhere. There was so
many about he kept a sack on his plough and chucked 'em into that. Some of

* Jack Donaldson and Arthur Postle were both Australian athletes.

Percy Pepper, left, and Frank Moon, approximately 1907 (F. Moon).

the farmers threshed their own maize and the *Tanjil** picked it up with other lots all along the Tambo and took it all across Lake King to Bairnsdale.

Our family went hop-picking at Briagolong and I can remember Mum and Dad would be each side of the bin, and Dora and me were small and we'd be on the side plucking the hops off. We got up on the pole, Dora and me, and threw them off. We'd camp on the river or live in huts on the farms at picking times.

Dad went shearing with Granny's husband, Grandfather John Conolly, and they worked the sheds together. If one got the contract 'e gave work to the other. There was a few of them did that; they helped each other. If one had a bit in his pocket he'd share it. John was a great shearer—he worked on the farm at Ramahyuck before he come out—and he could do his hundred

* *Tanjil*: One of the first paddle steamers working between Sale and Bairnsdale.

54

sheep a day by the blades. There was a gang of these fellas and if you couldn't do your hundred you was no good in the gang. They had Herb Murray, Walter McCreedie and Donald Cameron. He was a cunnin' shearer that one, Don Cameron. Off would come 'is boots and he'd put his feet under the sheep's belly and rub 'em along and know which ones was baldy, and he'd grab it and that'd save him shearing all round it. The rest of the shearers couldn't make out 'ow he was downin' them. He was the ringer in the shed, beating old Conolly and me old bloke, and when that shed was finished he told it to Walter McCreedie. Next shed Walter reckoned he could beat Don, so he'd rub his hand under the sheep's belly and, when they was baldy, he'd nick the ear, get a bit of wool off it and when it come to shearing he picked the ones 'e marked. He was the ringer, the top shearer in the shed then.

Sometimes when the Dad was away I stayed with Grandfather and Granny Thorpe; 'course I had cousins there now. Julie and Henry had Reggie and we'd go to school through the scrub and bush; you couldn't even see the sea from the hill in them days.

Grandfather and Uncle Henry dug the graves sometimes at the cemetery and we used to go over and watch. Anyway, an old sea captain got buried there and when he was put in 'e wasn't facin' the sea so they had to take 'im up later. Well, Reggie and me knocked off 'is name plate and buried it in a hole. Do you think old Billy and Henry didn't go crook? They asked us, did we see the plate and what we did with it; we told them we buried it but wouldn't tell them where. Gee we got a hiding for it. I think it was poor old Captain Heggarty's plate.

There's a tomb there in the Lakes Entrance cemetery belongs to a bloke used to come to see Grandfather every week. He'd come up in the boat, but it was always late and by the time he got to Lakes Entrance from Stratford 'e would be stone drunk. He'd stagger up towards Grandfather's place but he never could make it past that cemetery. Something took him through that gate and he used to go to sleep, right in the middle of the place, and he'd wake up in the morning and get out of there as fast as he could get.

The fruit trees Grandfather planted when he first got his ground had beautiful fruit on 'em and were a terrible temptation to Reggie and me, and we'd nick any soon as they got ripe and old Granny always wanted them for cookin'. She was a real mean old sheila and didn't like us to get the fruit. We weren't allowed to go in the paddock where they were, so Reggie and me fixed up a shanghai with a little spear on it and some string to shoot the apples with, see? Grandfather caught us sometimes, but he'd just say 'Come on boys, eat as many as you like. Granny can't use 'em all, she's got enough for the chutney in there now.'

We all went to church and Sunday School at St John's on the mission and it was always a great day for us kids. Granny was a big fat woman and by the time she got in the buggy with Grandfather there wasn't much room left for many others, and Reggie and me ran alongside. When we got to the lakeside, Grandfather would make a fire and then put green boughs on it so the smoke could be seen from the settlement and someone would come over the lake for us in a boat. The funny part was when Granny tried to get in the boat to cross over to the station. We'd watch Grandfather get in first to help her into it, then when she got in—bang—down it would go almost under the water . . . we always waited to see it go right under.

Rev. John Bulmer would hold the services but Captain Howe was the manager. While the service was on and the singin', with Auntie Allie playing the organ, Reggie Thorpe, Dingo Hood, the Moffatts and meself would duck outta the church and go bird-nesting. Captain Howe always seemed to see us and he'd come up behind us cracking his stock-whip and telling us to get back in that church. One crack of that whip and we were off.

The fishin' was good there at the lake—mullet, bream, flathead and prawns. When I went floundering with the old people—I'd be about ten—they made their own light. Old Grandfather Billy collected what they called candle-bark off the trees. It would curl up and be about as thick as your finger and sometimes in long pieces. He'd put some stringy-bark in the centre and bind it on to a lump of tree about five feet long. He'd light that and hold it up in the water and you could see into the water for ten feet around while they went after the flounder, using a length of fencing wire to stick the fish with.

One of the jobs Grandfather did when Lake Tyers was open to the sea was crossing the mail and the passengers in a boat, and the drivers of the coach had to swim the horses across and harness them in another coach on the other side. Sometimes that entrance there stayed open for three or four months, same as today.

In between the seasons on his little farm Grandfather went out to the old Bruthen road in his horse and buggy to find trees to split, easy trees, 'cos he wasn't too young then. He'd cut them in six-foot-six lengths, load 'em on to a cart and take the timber to sell it to the townspeople and the farmers.

About 1910 Uncle Henry put his mark on a tree down along the old Lake Tyers road and it was still there forty years later. He cut the bark off the tree with 'is tomahawk, got his hand real wet and stuck it in charcoal and blackened it, then he pressed 'is hand on to the tree where he cut the bark away. That mark would never wash away and every time we went camping down there we'd all look to see his mark.

Uncle Henry and Grandfather killed the kangaroos for meat for our mob. They'd skin 'im, whip out the back-bone and hang the meat up for a coupla days and it was beautiful eating. Whites used to eat the kangaroo too y'know because they were the same as the Aboriginal people—they were gettin' very little money in those days and if there was a few kids about, they had to feed 'em didn't they? 'Course you wasn't supposed to kill kangaroos then or the wallabies, but they all poached on these animals because they got a bit of money from the skins too. Scrape the skins out and dry 'em and take them way in the gully they did. After they got enough they took 'em to Jackson's Tannery in Bairnsdale where the bridge goes across. They'd sell them under the lap. Uncle Henry and Grandfather, too, but Dad didn't because he had work on the timber and doin' some fencin' about the place. He got half a crown for a ton of wood, worked out four feet high and five feet wide. The Thorpes stripped wattle bark too for tanning the skins and sold it to the buyer who come up from Melbourne. They had to let the bark dry out and then roll it up and sell it for three bob a ton. They were lucky to get two bob for a kangaroo skin.

Us little kids knew all about the wild cherry trees and the white kids come with us to pick them. We'd have good feeds off the trees too; the cherry was very sweet and as big as your nail but the trouble was the kangaroos would come along and pull the branches down and eat them. Other times we pulled the bark off the sugar gums and there's a little white speck in there and we'd stick our fingers on it and eat that. It's sweet and that's how it got the name of sugar-gum tree. There used to be yams about then too but we never liked them—but we took 'em home to Grandfather and he'd say, 'That's good

Tribesman spearing fish by candle-bark, 1896 (The La Trobe Collection, State Library of Victoria).

tukka.' He loved his feed of yams but there's none now; the cattle have destroyed all that.

All the people loved Lake Tyers and looked on that place as their home. Grandfather and Granny Thorpe went there with us kids when the school holidays were on. Not on the settlement, that wasn't allowed, but sometimes when the lake was closed the Aborigines come over the high sands from the settlement and camped in the bush overlookin' the beach there. They'd dig a hole for fresh water and there were plenty of hummocks with basket grass for the women to make their baskets. This was Grandfather's favourite camp. I was only a little fella in them days. The Peppers and the Thorpes would all be there and the young ones had to ride their horses back into Lakes Entrance every day to feed the chooks.

There was a big mahogany tree we camped under and there was always plenty for us to do, like going down the hill to the water edge and turn the rocks over and get the feather-leg crabs, and we could fish and climb trees, look for birds' nests. What we liked maybe most of all was listening to the old people talk. Grandfather's stories were the best of all. We learnt how to talk the language and the old tribal stories, like when the old clever bloke of the tribe threw a handful of ashes at a tribesman and said, 'You turn into a *gama-gama*'—that's a black cockatoo. He showed us the white fungus from gum-trees they used to keep the fires going with.

There was the story about the Hairy Man; it could be a man or a woman, but the Aborigines called it a man. Some called it *nargun*. It was a bad thing anyway. It was seven feet tall and went out at night to hunt the children and eat them. One night the Hairy Man come to the camp to get more children but it couldn't get in because of all the fires set around. While that *nargun* stamped around to get in to the children his feet got burnt. In the morning one of the Aborigines said when he saw the marks, 'What blackfella's track is this?' The people could see it wasn't one of their marks and they knew it was the Hairy One, so they followed the tracks around and they led to the top of Tooloo. Well some were frightened and didn't go any further and went back to the camp. Three of the tribesmen who kept on going were Big Charlie, Big Joe and Short Harry—'course that wasn't their names then, they had their tribal names—and they followed the Hairy Man to a cave. Now there were still other tribesmen with them three blokes and they started bangin' the *nargun* with their waddies, knockin' at it with the *nulla-nullas* and pokin' their spears into it. There was legs and arms flying everywhere, but they couldn't get the Hairy Man out of the hole. Short Harry, because 'e was the shortest, had to crawl into the cave after the *nargun*. He grabbed a foot but there were so many legs and feet dangling about he wasn't sure if it was the *nargun*'s, so he yelled out, 'What blackfella's foot is this?' One of the tribesmen said it was his, so Short Harry kept grabbin' until nobody answered, then they all knew it was the Hairy One's leg. He hung on and the Aborigines cut the Hairy Man's ham-string with reed and bone knives. That's how they finished off the *nargun*.

Clive Hood 'Hockey', born at Lake Tyers 1908. Alec Moffatt, born at Lake Tyers 1910, approximately 1914.

Blackfellas Track was just a wallaby track when the old people used to go on it to Bairnsdale and beyond. It's in the State Forest now and the kangaroos still come out at night to feed there. Someone's changed the name to Black-fellows Drive; there's a notice-board there. It should still be Blackfellas Track on that board, because that is what it was.

One night I was sitting with Grandfather on top of Blay's Hill—called Davern Drive now—and it was a bright night, a full moon, and I said to him,

57

'Grandpa I'll tell you a little yarn now, about that moon', and he said, 'Go on, Willie', —'course that's my second name—and I said

> Pretty moon I see you float
> Up above so high
> Tell me moon who put you there
> And makes you shine so bright.

Grandfather said, 'Who did that, Willie?', so I told him.

> God put me here to shine so bright
> To give out gentle light
> So you can see the stars at night.

When Billy Thorpe had his little farm at Lakes Entrance there was a murder committed at Merrangbaur Hill where he had worked for Roadknights. There were two white blokes camped in the gully thereabouts and they went up to the house to play cards. There were a few of them playing and one of these blokes from the camp began to lose and the more they chiacked him, the more he lost, getting real wild, see? Well he got beaten properly and when those two men went back to their camp, the one that lost his money was ribbed about it by his mate. He kept at him and got him so mad, he picked up his tomahawk and clouted him on the back of his head—killed him. Well he stuck the dead bloke between some logs and cleared off to Bairnsdale. He made a mistake when he sold their blankets and the tent, because they found blood on them and the police were called in and he was questioned about it. The police went back to the camp at Merrangbaur Hill and found the dead bloke.

In February of 1896 two pressmen who worked for the Weekly Times *in Melbourne arranged to go to the Gippsland Lakes for their holidays, not to confine themselves to the steamship routes through the Great Lakes, but to proceed to Tyers because this lake was little known by the general public.*

They travelled by train to Sale, from there in the steamer to the new Entrance, where they boarded the coach for Lake Tyers on the roughest road ever experienced by the men, through scrub and forest tracks. The driver knew his two passengers were journalists and interested in news, so he took them to the scene of the murder near Roadknight's Merrangbaur House. The young man Strange had recently been executed in the Melbourne Gaol for the murder of his friend.

The camp had been little disturbed since the night of the murder. The tent and any personal belongings had been removed but the tent sticks were still standing. The utensils were still where they had been placed after being cleaned and put away when the men had finished their last meal. The frying-pan had two tin plates on top, ready for use. A 'paperman' had taken a plate and the pressmen were told he was ready to make a deal with showmen for its purchase.

The scene of the murder was an out-of-the-way place and the two Melbourne men believed this was the reason the camp-site had remained undisturbed. They saw the original slab-hut at Merrangbaur which was in quite good condition.[3]

The 1914–18 War

UNCLE HENRY THORPE WINS THE M.M.

UNCLE HENRY THORPE ENLISTED IN GIPPSLAND FOR THE 1914–18 WAR. HE won a Military Medal but he was killed just before armistice. This is his story:

> 'Corporal Henry Thorpe won the M.M. He was a half-caste aborigine born about October 1887 at Orbost, Victoria, the son of William and Lilian Thorpe. He enlisted at Sale on 12th. February 1916 and embarked for overseas service in April. He joined the 7th Battalion and saw action with his unit in France and Belgium. He was wounded in action at Pozières on 21st. August 1916 and again at Bullecourt on 29th. April 1917 and was appointed Lance Corporal on 10th. January 1917.

> 'During operations near Ypres on 4th–5th October 1917, Thorpe displayed great courage and initiative in mopping up enemy dugouts and pill-boxes. He was conspicuous for his courage and leadership in the capture of the 7th. Battalion objective and he both handled his men with skill and materially assisted his company commander. For his example and disregard of all danger, which served to inspire the men he commanded, he was promoted Corporal on 5th. October and awarded the M.M. on 31st. October. Thorpe met his end at Lihons Wood, south-west of Vauvillers, in a costly advance on the afternoon of 9th. August 1918. The 7th Battalion had been caught with its left flank exposed to severe enemy fire owing to the failure of a flanking unit to support it, and it was here that a stretcher-bearer found Thorpe shot in the stomach. He asked for water but the bearer refused, knowing the further harm that would be caused to his injuries. The bearer made him as comfortable as possible and took the casualty he already had to the dressing station. Returning for Thorpe, the bearer found him in agony, apparently caused through some misguided samaritan having given him a drink. He died shortly after reaching the dressing station and was buried . . . in the Heath Cemetery at Harbonnières . . .'[1]

Lakes Entrance War Memorial, front and back. Last name—Thorpe, H.

That was a fact about someone giving Uncle Henry some water, because our people talked to some of the blokes who come back and knew Henry. If you look on the War Memorial at Lakes Entrance you'll see his name there.

Billy Rawlings was another Aboriginal who got the M.M. He got killed in the same action as Henry. One of his sisters was Reg Saunder's mother—he was in the next war—his youngest sister became Lionel Rose's* grandmother.

* Lionel Edmund Rose was born in Warragul, Gippsland, in 1948. His boxing titles include:
  1963—Australian Amateur Flyweight.
  1964—Victorian Amateur Bantamweight.
  1966—Australian Professional Bantamweight.
  1968—World Bantamweight Title, won in Japan.
  Lionel was awarded the M.B.E. in 1968.

Herbert Murray.

Julia Thorpe (née Scott), Braggin Scott, Katherine McCreedie (née Scott), 1919 (The La Trobe Collection, State Library of Victoria).

Dad was in Warrnambool and he enlisted there and Georgie Rose was a Warrnambool boy and he joined up with Dad but he was too young, just seventeen, and Dad put his weights up so he did not go overseas. That Georgie was Lionel's grandfather. Walter McCreedie and Herb Murray were another couple who went to the war; they linked up in England with the old man. Walter McCreedie's sister was the widow of Phillip Pepper, the Dad's brother. Herb Murray married my wife Ethel's sister Eva.

Well when Herbie and Walter were on the train at Lindenow to go off, someone said to Walter, 'Aren't y' frightened to go to the war?' He pulled his little Bible out of his pocket and said, 'No, that'll stop all the bullets and fetch me back home safe.' He come home all right.

Walter was a real clown; he'd do anything for a laugh. They met Dad in England and one day they borrowed a pair of kilts off the Scottish Regiment and dressed Walter McCreedie up as a black Scotchman and, when the soldiers seen him there, they couldn't make 'im out. 'Well, I'm a McCreedie and I'm entitled to dress up in me native uniform. I'm the Black Scotchman,' he told 'em. When they got back home to Gippsland and the story went round, Walter was always called the Scotch Blackfella.

Another time in Sale, when there used to be a lot of Indians about, he got one of them to put a turban on 'im. Well they wound it round and round his head till it stuck right up. He was a big fat fella, Walter was then. He went off and mixed himself up with some other Indians walkin' about Sale, then he went into the bar where Dad and Grandfather Conolly were with Herb Murray and old Charlie Green. They reckoned they knew all them Indians about the place and they kept lookin' at this fat fella, so at last they went over to 'im and o' course he turned out to be McCreedie, the Indian. They said he was a man of all flags, as the sayin' goes.

Walter married Braggin Scott's sister Katherine, called Katie. Now there was in that family Braggin, Thomas, Julia and Katie and their father was James Scott, called Jamsie. He had married Billy Login's widow, Mary, and those four children were from that marriage. Jamsie was a real funny blackfella and Grandfather used to talk about him a lot. One time they were doin' the fencin' at the mission and Jamsie was s'posed to be with them but instead he was down after the swans, so they went to see him. There he was in amongst the tussocks, turnin' somersaults and rollin' round over and over and jumpin' around on his knees. See, the swans are peculiar inquisitive birds and they got closer and closer to see what was going on. Jamsie kept watching them and he'd roll around again. The swans were comin' in closer, stickin' their necks out, and at last one of them left the bunch and come in nearer to Jamsie. Next minute he jumps up, throws 'is boomerang along the water, knocks the swan's head off and dives into the lake. He grabbed the head of the swan and swam along with just the swan's head stickin' up out of the water. Jamsie got in amongst the other swans, grabbed their legs and got as many as he wanted.

The Scotts went to the Ramahyuck school, same as the Peppers did. Braggin was a beauty too. Dad and Herbie Murray said Braggin read anything he got his hands on. He knew all about everything and told the people what he read in a funny way. He used to try to make himself smart amongst the others and he'd say things like, 'You know boys, the plumage on that swan's wings is brilliant.' He'd have you laughin' all day, that man. Braggin was born the same year Nathaniel died.

When Dad was away at the war I learnt a bit about farmin' from Grand-

Christmas card from Percy in
France to his family in 1917;
'May the coming days be your
happiest days,
And your happiest days be the
longest'.

father Thorpe, learnt how to plough with him steering the plough while I drove the two horses. I was older then but Grandpa still told me about the early days and one time we went down on to the Ninety-Mile Beach for 'im to show me one of the old tribe camp-sites, where the sand was naturally scooped out and completely surrounded by scrub and trees. There was banksias, pittosporum, honeysuckle, callistomen and ferns covered over with creepers. There were some kanooka and dogwoods there—you gotta be careful when you muck around with dogwoods, you get barcoo-rot and it takes a lot to get rid of it, you get sores and lumps from dogwoods and it makes you pretty sick. You get ticks off kanooka bush, so you put metho on and that fixes them.

I've been back to that campin' place and you can almost see the old people there eating their tukka and listenin' to the sea roarin' on to the white sand below—the smell of the trees about there—and I could just about smell the smoke from the fire and their meat cookin'. Then I remember somethin' else he told me that spoils that pitcher; he said, 'The old people told the young ones, when they travelled the beach or open forest, never walk in front of a white man, always walk behind.'

See, they got so frightened of the white men they thought they'd get shot and it put the fear in 'em. Anyway, they'd run as soon as they saw a *lohan* comin'.

You see the reason Dad joined up in Warrnambool was he had taken us there when he was working. He had to go where he could find work, so he put us at Lake Condah Aboriginal Station until he was able to get a house for us on the Hopkins River. When they wanted men for the war he didn't tell Mum he was thinkin' of joining up, he just went and did it. I can remember us kids cryin' when we found out he was going away. When he left, Mum took us back to Lakes Entrance where Sammy and me lived most of the time with Grandfather Thorpe. Mum and the girls lived at the Lakes and after a while come to Grandfather's too.

Dad wasn't a cook in the Army. He was in the front lines fighting. You see, the time he had his fingers caught in the winch he lost two fingers, but the Army tested him to see if he could manage the rifle and he was all right so they sent him off. He fought in the same battle in France as Henry Thorpe. Dad sent me home post cards to keep for him and I've still got some. One was of a Cathedral with the Virgin Mary on the top. He told us she was pointing to England, then overnight something happened and in the morning the men saw she was pointing to Germany and that was when the tide turned and they got the Germans on the run.

When he first went away the English people called our blokes 'six bob a day tourists'. My Dad only got six bob a day and he took the shillin' and left the rest for Mum to keep the family on. We used to get bush tukka to help feed us all. Us young boys went out in the bush with Grandfather and he always took his dog Dash along. Old Dash knew his game and he'd look for the wombat burras and he'd start barkin' to let us know when he found one. Dash was a little fox terrier and could fit easily in the wombat hole, turn round and get out again. Well, while he was in the hole, us kids would put our ears to the ground and listen to see if Dash was barkin' in there; sometimes he'd rush out and so would a wombat. More often Grandfather would dig 'em out and Old Jack Bennett, a white bloke, sometimes went with us on weekends and he'd dig too. The wombats were usually about four feet underground.

61

When we got home the men scraped them down with a piece of shaped up tin, get all the hair off—and the tics. The skin was as tough as a pig's. The wombats were dropped into kero tins of boiling water and after that Grandfather cut the animals up and put 'em in a cask of brine and kept turnin' them. When it was ready, the meat was hung up and it looked like a ham, the dead spit of bacon, see?

It was beautiful meat. The old people fried it or boiled it—it was a good meal and there's nothin' wrong with eating them either. Those animals are clean, not like a pig. The wombat's a terrible animal where there's a wire fence and costs the farmers pounds and pounds because one pull with his claw and he could break the wire right along a fence. They paid five bob a skull to get rid of 'em.

SCHOOL WITH COUSIN REGGIE
THORPE

We all walked to school from Grandfather's little farm. You know where the boat ramp is at Lakes Entrance and the road that comes out towards the back of the lake? Well right on that corner was where our school was. We'd wag school sometimes but the teacher didn't mind. He knew we had a long way to walk. If it was raining we had to walk round the road instead of through the scrub tracks. The girls always wore button up boots to school and the boys went barefooted in the dry weather. All the white boys were the

Pepper family, approximately 1912. *(left to right) Back:* **Dora, Percy with Sam.** *Front:* **Gwen, Alice, Sarah, Lucy, Phillip.**
(Lena was born later.)

Photo of Phillip given by Percy, Phillip's son, Lindsay 'Jumbo'.

same out there in the bush—same as us—no boots. In the wet weather we tied our boots around our necks so they wouldn't get wet and wear out, then they'd last us a lot longer. They were good hobnailed boots they had for us with hard leather. Sometimes in the wet seasons we wouldn't get to school before ten o'clock.

There was an old white bloke called Frank Duffy who took all the groceries round the town on the horse and dray and us little kids helped him and got a penny or tuppence. Some days we'd do a bit of bird nesting on the way to school or chasin' rabbits. There were a lot of poddy calves about and we'd round 'em up and ride these calves around for a while before settin' off on the track through the scrub for school.

One time at school Reggie Thorpe and me was playing wars with the other kids and we said we were the Australians and the kids who were the Germans tried to lock us outside the school gate. I pitched a stick that went straight through the school window and smashed it. They told us we had to pay for the window but we didn't have the money so Mum went to see the teachers. And Grandfather Billy Thorpe told the officers at the Army recruiting depot the trouble we got ourselves into and somehow everything got fixed up because our fathers were both at the war. But the kids at school were nice kids and we all got on together.

There was a good white bloke livin' there called Tas Aimes. He was mixed up with the Aboriginal people from the early days. He had a boat and was a fisherman during the war and he would give fish to Sammy, my brother, and me and Reggie Thorpe, our cousin, to take home to Grandfather. I'd stick the fish in me school bag to take home. Tas gave fish to the white kids, too, who lived in the bush. When he died I went to his funeral. I felt for that man. He was a real good sort he was.

CHAPTER EIGHT

After the War: Friends of the Family and Sport

A SOLDIER SETTLEMENT BLOCK
AT KOO-WEE-RUP

WHEN DAD COME BACK FROM THE 1914–18 WAR AND WAS DISCHARGED, HE applied for a block of ground at Koo-wee-rup Swamp, forty miles out of Melbourne. He got this block of sixty-five acres all told and of course he didn't know too much about farmin', but when we moved to the farm Georgie Rose come there too and worked on the farm. We all helped each other, with Georgie comin' along behind me planting the spuds and Dad and Mother culling them.

The house there wasn't ready and we lived with another returned soldier in his house and he boarded with us there. See how they helped each other? The man who had the contract for building the houses on the Soldier Settlement blocks come up from Melbourne to inspect the work every Monday and I got work with him those times. We had brought our horse and jinker with us from the lakes, and I'd pick him up in that at the station and drive 'im all round the different farms and he'd give me fourteen shillins every Monday. I gave Mum twelve and kept two bob for going to the pictures. I would have been about thirteen years old then.

BUILDING A HOUSE, CLEARING
THE LAND, FARMING SPUDS

When our house was finished and we moved in, we saw the timber shrank after a while and the builders had to come back and they put a length of timber over the openings to stop the draught. The house was built three foot off the ground and when we got the floods the water didn't get inside.

The returned soldiers helped us out with some teams of horses and we

The first photo taken of Koo-wee-rup township. Rossiter Road from Alexander Avenue, 1901 (Tom Burhop).

64

ploughed up pretty near all the ground. When we was ploughin' you'd see all the seagulls swarmin' along behind us, scoopin' up all the worms and insects, grubs and things. It was a beautiful sight too, all those white birds following the tractor. Anyway we got a loan of an iron-age planter too, and I went to a school every weekend with other sons of returned men and we learnt farming and how to cut the spuds for planting. The government put a lot of the returned soldiers on blocks at the Koo-wee-rup swamps.

> *'The Great Koo-wee-rup Swamp . . . so far as the history of the white or the tradition of the black Australian goes, the Swamp was always a swamp. To the black inhabitants of the northern and south western territories, it was of evil repute. Their tradition tells of a monster invariably called by the different tribes the bunyip or* tooridin, *which made its home in the dense ti-tree and watery wastes of the district. This myth was neither flesh, fish nor fowl. It was described as a little of each, with nothing in common with any, for no living being, white or black, saw it swim, walk or fly. It simply existed in a mighty roar at night "resembling that of a lion". How the blacks came to compare the sound with the roar of a lion is not explained, but it is sufficient to say that they gave the Swamp a wide berth. A little of their superstition seems to have been transmitted to the early settlers around its margins, for even the white man held the watery wastes in awe. Stories of men being lost in its dense scrub and never seen again, of mobs of cattle being swallowed up in its morasses, were told with bated breath . . .'*

The Swamp remained shrouded in mystery right up to the late eighties of last century. It was then that two enterprising American brothers, the Chaffeys of Mildura fame, were first to see the possibilities of a drainage scheme 'to reclaim the land and fit it for closer settlement'. The offer they made to the State for the Swamp was refused, but the Government realised the possibilities of reclamation.

After the crash of the land boom in Victoria the Government 'conceived the idea of establishing Village Settlements' and a swamp reclamation would be a means of employment for men who had lost their money, homes and jobs.

One of the many Koo-wee-rup Swamp floods. *(left to right)* Percy, Tom George (a bike-rider) and Phillip.

Pepper family on the farm. The driver was R. Stevens, later a well known bike-rider, 1923.

AGRICULTURE AT KOO-WEE-RUP SWAMP IN THE 1920s TO 1930s

Bullock teams cleared the swamps for the drainage system and worked on the ti-tree scrub, clearing the land for the soldier settlement blocks. A triangular outrigger-type roller was constructed, using steel railway rails for the frame. As the bullock team dragged the outrigger through the scrub, the tall ti-tree was bent over first, then rolled (Tom Burhop).

After ridding the farm of acres of ti-tree scrub often 20 feet high, teams of horses were used to cultivate the ground, manuring and planting. Phillip is shown with horses, Jess and Gyp.

Acres of potato plants thriving between floods. The Burhop homestead is in the background. In the very early days, potatoes were planted by hand (Tom Burhop).

The potatoes matured successfully in 1933 and the diggers have laid them in rows ready for culling and bagging. The workers are members of The Little Brother Movement, who migrated from England in the 1920s (Tom Burhop).

The same land under flood in 1934. The Burhops used the 'barrel and pole' method of transportation. Forty square miles of Koo-wee-rup Swamp were under water (Tom Burhop).

Roy Dixon helps with digging and bagging at Peppers farm. The homestead is in the background.

'When the project of drainage works for the "Great Koo-wee-rup Swamp" was first put forward, the "Doubting Thomas's" of those days, shook their heads dolefully, and declared that the drainage of the Swamp was an utter impossibility . . . it would merely make room for the saltwaters of Western Port Bay to take its place.' The draughtsmen, under the late C. Catani, engineer for roads and bridges, drew up a scheme of drainage. The area to be dealt with covered 250 square miles of unexplored country, fed by three rivers and a score of creeks, distributing their waters over 85,000 acres of timber and jungle. Part of the scheme included fifty-four miles of main drains, but the cost was too high and the scheme was modified. Had the original scheme been carried out, the drainage of the Swamp would have been successful, 'as it is, over thirty years have elapsed, and there are portions of it not drained yet', a journalist wrote in 1923.

The first section of reclamation was at the Koo-wee-rup end in 1890 and hundreds of unemployed men were sent to the Swamp from Melbourne. They worked in mud ditches up to their waists in water and became known as 'the muck shifters'.

Three years later the work had advanced enough for the Government to have the first land sale but only on odd blocks could any building be attempted. Everything had a habit of disappearing beneath the surface and the men could never agree on the depth of the mud and peat. They placed planks across the mud for easier travelling which was not altogether successful as 'Bill used to relate how he found Paddy's hat on the mud bank, and on picking it up he saw Paddy's head under it, and he gave him a lecture for being so foolish as to step off the planking. Paddy defended himself by replying that Bob had disappeared down the hole and he had only got down to give Bob a hold of his legs.'

The Aborigines must have overcome their fear of the tooridin *on the Swamp because Kooweerup roughly translated means the home of the blackfish, and that is what it was. After the 'tapping of the Bunyip River with the main drain, water ceased to flow over that section east of the Bunyip drain. Throughout the whole area blackfish were left stranded in shallow pools.' The local residents scooped up the fish in buckets and hundreds of boxes of the fish were sent to Melbourne for sale.*[1]

HE OLD SWASTIKA CAFÉ

There was an old café in the Koo-wee-rup town owned by George Colvan and he called it the Swastika Café and next to this eat-up joint he had a bike shop and he called the bikes the Swastika* too. It's all burned down now but, anyway, in them days, he had an old Ford car he took passengers round in, and he hired it to Dad to take us to Melbourne to see the Prince of Wales. They let off 3,000 pigeons that day. Well in that Ford there was George Colvan driving, Dad, Mum, Dora, Gwennie, Sam, Lena and meself. We had a great day and comin' home along the swamp the fog was so bad Dad got out to lead George along the edge of the drain. We were all so cold when we got back to the Swastika Café Dad bought a bottle of O.T. to warm us all up. It's a real hot sort of cordial you mix with water.

Quail shootin' was popular with Melbourne men and the policeman at the Swamp paid me one pound every time I guarded our stubble paddock (where

---

* The swastika is an ancient religious symbol dating from the Stone Age. Before the rise of Hitler, who adopted it and therefore brought it into disfavour, the swastika was a lucky sign.

The Swastika Café on the right (Tom Burhop).

the oats were taken out) for his father to shoot in. Dad had to put a notice on our paddock to keep the shooters out—they'd come with their dogs to flush out the quail.

Entertainment for the returned soldiers' families was house parties in each other's homes and everyone had to do something, like sing or tell a story. They were good times.

One time a bloke named Jack had three water commissioners in his car and he crossed the train line in front of the train comin' in to Koo-wee-rup. The three men were killed, but Jack grabbed hold of the kero light on the train and straddled the cow-catcher and hung on. He was all right except for a few cuts and scratches.

FLOODS

We had three rattling good seasons on the farm and the old man was sitting pretty, then he had a couple of crook ones. The floods cleaned us out, but we set up again, like all the other soldiers on their blocks.

We had good times with the bad. Everyone loved sport and Georgie Rose was a great runner, so Dad started to train him while we were at the Swamp. I bought a bike, a Swastika, and we trained on a seventy-yard track and a half-mile track; Dad would say, 'Get riding' and off I'd go, and when I got even with Georgie Rose the Dad would fire the gun and Georgie ran down the track with me on me racer beside him.

FOOT RACES AND CYCLE RACES

When the Koo-wee-rup Sports was on about 1922 it finished up as Pepper's Sports Day. My mother won the married women's race, my sister won her race and the old bloke, that's the Dad, won the Buffers' race and Georgie Rose won the seventy-five yards and the two hundred and twenty. He was a very smart man, Georgie, he wasn't big, about Lionel's build, and if he said he wanted to do anything, he would do it and do it well, and in a race he was always determined to win—he always tried. He was pretty good, too. He won the Gift at Bairnsdale and Leongatha.

We had a lot of cycle races in those days and Percy Osborn is one bloke you couldn't forget. We had a race down Warrnambool way that we were in.

(left to right) Phillip, Georgie Rose, Sinclair Mills.

Percy Osborn put up a good performance in getting into tenth place in the Warrnambool to Melbourne road race. There were 200 participants, and

68

from the start of the race to the finish, it was estimated that 150,000 people witnessed the race. 'Cycling is evidently reviving again both in the city and the country, and judging by the interest displayed in Melbourne and the large amounts in prize money it is gaining the prestige which it had twenty years ago.'[2]

While we were on the farm Dad bought a bike shop at Tynong, that's between Bunyip and Nar-Nar-Goon, and that helped us along when things were bad.

At a meeting attended by 300 ex-soldiers, including men from Koo-wee-rup and Tooradin, a pessimistic description was given of the soldier settlements. It was said that because of the excessive charges for land and improvements, 'many capable and industrious soldier settlers are unable to meet all financial obligations to the Closer Settlement Board . . . it is impossible for the most hard-working soldier settler to make headway under present conditions.' It was proposed that the Act should be amended, under which they held land, 'to provide that interest on advances should be abolished . . .' The proposal was defeated. At this time, in 1923, the Government had settled 9816 men on land in Victoria and had blocks for a further 749.[3]

One time when Dad was in Melbourne he saw Charlie Foster. He was one of the boys who was with the Peppers at the Ramahyuck mission until they had to leave. The poor fella had gone blind, so Dad brought him back to Koo-wee-rup for a while. Charlie loved the farm and he'd go out and feel the grass; he'd be down on his knees and he'd say, 'That's nice high grass, about six inches,' then he'd put his hands on the bushes of peas and say, 'They're good peas.' Charlie Foster knew the different grasses—the clover or the rye—by just feelin' them; he was that smart. He knew which cows was good and which was poor. After a while he had to go back to the hospital in Melbourne and I can't remember anything more about Charlie after that. We never seemed to hear anything about him.

Percy Pepper's shop.

Our worst year at the Swamp was the year Mum died. She had been sick for years with consumption and it killed her before she was forty. That was in 1924. Mum had thirteen operations and Dr Hagenauer was the man who took care of her, Rev. Hagenauer's son. One time Mum was in one room at the hospital and Dr Hagenauer was treating Dad in the other. Dad had caught his fingers in a winch when he was working on one of the boats in Gippsland as the cook, before they had the farm. Dr Hagenauer was good to the Aborigines. Well that shows how long Mum was sick for. That year she died, the farm got knocked twice with floods, well bad floodin' I mean.

When residents were prosecuted for non-payment of the drainage rates it was declared that the time chosen for such action was ill-advised as the district had just emerged from two of the most disastrous floods in the history of Koo-wee-rup and the stories of the farmers' losses were well known. The State Rivers and Water Supply Commission was accused of having 'failed lamentably in accomplishing what it set out to do, viz., construct an effective drainage scheme in the flood areas of the Koo-wee-rup Swamp . . .'[4]

After Mum died, Dad stayed on the block with us, but it wasn't the same any more. It was a terrible struggle to keep the place goin' and after a while Auntie Allie and Auntie Emily come down and took the family, except me, back to Grandfather Thorpe, and Gwennie went to school there at Lakes Entrance.

The Commonwealth Government granted some relief to soldier settlers by writing off five million pounds, bringing the Commonwealth's share of losses to more than ten million pounds. It was believed that the contribution would be sufficient to cover more than half the total losses involved in the soldier settlement project.[5]

Dad helped Grandfather Thorpe with as much money as he could send, and things got a bit better too when the family got jobs in Bairnsdale and the Lakes. Dora was a maid for a while and when Gwennie left school she used to get odd jobs from different people around the town and had to walk home of a night to Thorpe's place. Dora walked too 'til she got a livin' in job.

Dad had to give up the farm at the Swamp in the finish but I stayed on for a while. Dad got a good job selling monumental stones—tombstones—in Melbourne and he'd come up to Koo-wee-rup to visit. He had that job for a long time. At one stage he got an order for a monument for Donald McCreedie and he felt crook about that because old Donald was his good friend, so he told 'em to make a real good one with good writin' on it. Well he had to go to the Repat. Hospital himself not long after and blow me if he don't knock into Donald McCreedie there. He said to him, 'Hey I've seen a monument for you,' and McCreedie said, 'Well that's good business, but I ain't payin' for it yet.'

Before we all left the Swamp Charlie Green* used to come down to the farm too. He was a great athlete, the best hurdle racer ever seen. He travelled to all the sports meetings. Percy Dahlsen of Bainsdale paid a bloke at Lake Tyers to train Charlie for hurdling and he took him to Stawell, where he won some of the hurdle races. He went to Echuca and Swan Hill too. Percy Dahlsen won a lot of money on Charlie, but he was a good sport with him. When Christmas come around he'd tell Charlie to bring his wife and kids to

* Charlie Green was one of the Aborigines painted by Percy Leason, see page 102.

town and he'd buy clothes for them, even a suit for Charlie and toys for the kids.

One time Dad got Charlie to Koo-wee-rup to give an exhibition. A bloke called Mark Williams was the starter and Charlie was that smart in the eyes, he'd look under his arm when Mark pulled the trigger and he'd be off before the sound of the gun. Bike-rider friends of mine, includin' Jack Fitzgerald, come to watch Charlie race, and Jack asked 'ow he got away so quick, and Charlie said, 'As soon as y'see that speck of smoke come out of that barrel, y'go.' Jack said he didn't have such a pair of powerful eyes. 'Well', said Charlie, 'that's the way I win me races.' Charlie Green would go over them hurdles like a bird flying.

He was keen on the water sports, a good swimmer and diver, and when the sports were held at the Lakes at Bairnsdale and Sale, Charlie would be there. One event was always popular and that was the Greasy Pole. This pole was fixed over the water and the competitors had to walk the whole length of it, collect a flag that was stuck out at the end and bring it back to the wharf. It wasn't easy of course, because the pole was well greased, but Charlie never missed getting that flag. When it was his turn to get on the pole, his cobber was there next to 'im with a hat full of sand—he'd drop it on the wharf and Charlie stood on it, rubbing his feet round, then he'd walk right along the pole and whip the flag off every time.

Another time all the people went to the diving competitions at Sale and Charlie lined up with the rest of 'em to go into the river. They'd given him a pair of nicks to wear and they were too big for 'im. Anyway off he went into the water and off come his nicks, so he dived under and swam right down aways where no one could see him. He come out amongst the reeds and by the time he got some clothes and went back to the competitions everyone was pretty worried about him. As he got close to where they all were, he could see a great fuss goin' on. The police was there and white blokes and blackfellas were all jumpin' in and out the water and a lot of yellin' was going on; well, he looked around for a bit, and watched his mates in the water splashing around. After a bit he walks up to a group watchin' the water and all the goin's on and he said, 'Hey what's the trouble?' One of the blokes said, 'We're all lookin' for you, Charlie.'

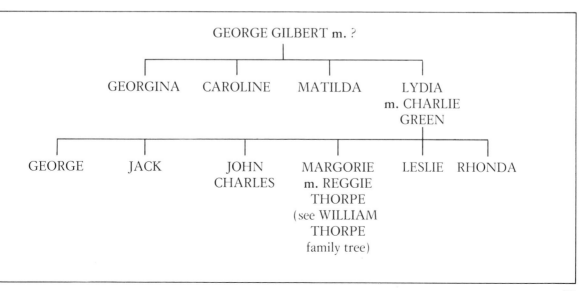

Charlie Green's parents were Lewis and Alexander, both full-blood Kurnai. Lewis was a Warn-a-ngatte man (Lake Tyers) and Alexander was from Port Albert. The family lived in a mia-mia when John Bulmer set up the mission. Lewis was a good athlete and also played the violin very well. He left his family at the mission and went to Sydney where he sang Sankey's Hymns in the streets. He did not return to Lake Tyers. Lewis died in New South Wales and Alexander died at the mission shortly after.

When Charlie grew older he worked as a whaler along the Gippsland and New South Wales coasts until he settled on the mission station and married Lydia Gilbert. Their daughter Margorie married Reggie Thorpe.

Charlie Green died of cancer at Orbost in 1955, aged about sixty.[6]

Con Edwards was another good sportsman. His family was the last lot to leave Ramahyuck when they closed that station down. His old father Billy had the tribal scars across his chest and arms. Well, they went to Lake Tyers to live and Con was a great footballer there and a good runner. Old Bob Wandin trained Con for the Stawell Gift. Bob Wandin was the station

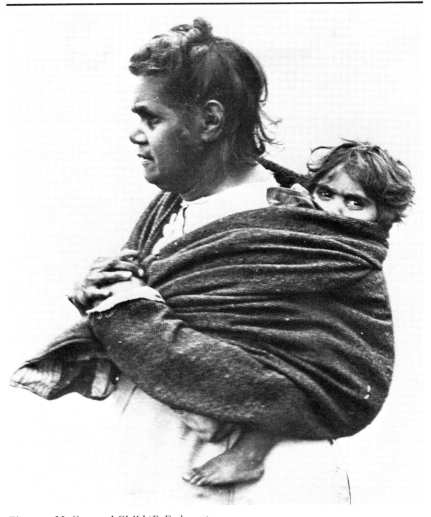

Florence Moffatt and Child (F. Endacott).

72

blacksmith and he used to temper the wedges for the white people outside and the station manager never knew about that. While I'm talkin' about the Wandin family, I'll just tell you here; they come from Coranderrk and one of them, Joe Wandin, we reckon he was the first Aboriginal teacher Victoria ever had—that is Education Department teacher. He passed the exams and got to be a teacher in Melbourne; a State School teacher.

In May 1901 Joseph Wandin was appointed pupil teacher to the Brunswick State School and in September he successfully passed the Education Department examinations and was appointed to West Brunswick State School with an increase in his salary. His wages were then 12s 6d a week and the Board agreed to assist him with board and lodging until he was able to maintain himself. He was then sixteen years old. In 1906 Joe was Junior Teacher at Badgers Creek S.S., Healesville. Various appointments followed until he retired in 1950 and his report reads, 'A skilful teacher who has faithfully given very good service for many years'.[7]

Con Edwards raced at all the sports round Gippsland and one year he won five Gifts. He was born at Ramahyuck and baptised Cornelius; we all called him Con. He knew all the stories about Ramahyuck and about all the people there. The family and the Peppers were friends and one of their children was called Percy Phillip, same as the Pepper brothers. A while after Uncle Henry Thorpe was killed, Con married Auntie Julia and they lived on at Lake Tyers. They had a good choir going there and Julia and Con sang in it. Florrie Foster was another who sang in the choir. She married Eddie Moffatt and they were the parents of Laurie and Foster and Sarah; they were connected with the Scotts because Sarah married Braggin.

There was another fella we called Muns. He was Jimmy Hammond and anything he did he asked for the money for the work. He kept nickin' off the station when he wasn't supposed to and that's how he learned the worth of money. When these blackfellas left the stations or didn't do as they were told by the manager, or gave any cheek—stood up for themselves—they got shifted away to another station. Sometimes a whole family was sent away or just one of a family, and if they were young men or women they mainly got sent to the homes.

Muns was a real devil, he would go off visiting the Aborigines he knew. Y'see, Muns and his brothers and sisters were orphans—first their mother died when they lived near Omeo and the sick father brought them to Lake Tyers, then he died, so that left the Aborigines Board in charge of them. After Muns finished his schooling, he worked on and off the station. When he went to Delegate on visits he'd walk straight through the bush along the kangaroo tracks with 'is dingo at his heels and wherever Muns slept his Dingo did too, right alongside him. Everyone liked Muns, white people and all, they'd give him a smoke. He went to Bega to live and he was quite happy to be there. I saw him at Bega twenty-odd years ago and he was a real nice old bloke.

Jimmy Hammond's father was Charles. As a child Charles had been taken from 'the blacks' and never allowed to associate with his tribe, the Brabuwooloong, at Swan Reach.

In 1863, when he was about twenty-five years old, he was with John Bulmer at Lake Tyers. Charley married and took his wife to live at Omeo where he worked for settlers and received usually around one pound a week. He

73

Living in a bark shelter on the lake (Nora Cochrane neé Forster).

applied for a grant of land to work and establish a farm for his family, but this was not approved.

For twenty years the Hammond family lived away from their own tribal people and Charley worked on the Tongio Station, supporting his family and having his children educated at the local state school.

In 1883 a settler asked that blankets be supplied to 'the family of blacks' who now had seven children to raise. They were destitute. The mother was ill and Charley could not earn enough money. Before the Board had given assistance, Charley's wife died, leaving a six-month-old baby. The eldest girl had a badly burned arm and was extremely ill and Charley could not keep going any longer and he agreed to return with his children to Lake Tyers.

Charley was a full-blood but his wife was not, so the children were termed 'half-caste', and under the law in 1890 they could not remain at Lake Tyers mission. Once again Charley tried to provide for his family, this time at Bruthen.

John Bulmer found the family in a bad way in 1891 and arrangements were made to send some of Charley's children to Industrial Schools in Melbourne. The eldest daughter was sent into service and Charley and young Jimmy were returned to Lake Tyers.

Charley Hammond had been ill for a long time. He died several months after his return to the mission at Lake Tyers.[8]

74

Living on or off a Reserve

GEORGE AND AGNUS THOMAS, MY WIFE ETHEL'S PARENTS, WENT TO Newmerella in about 1887*. They were there a few years when they lost all they owned in a fire, but George started again and set up a little cottage with a bark roof. He worked for Poddy Nixon, Peter's grandfather, driving his bullocks, and then he worked for David Morris who had a farm on the Snowy. David Morris had been one of the school teachers at Lake Tyers and he was always a good friend to the Aborigines. When Julia Thomas, the eldest girl, was fourteen she went to work for David's son Percy in his home, as a live-in servant for his family. There was six children and Julia lived and worked there with them till she married Henry Eaton, at Sale. After that wedding they rode their horses back to Grandfather Billy Thorpe's place, got them rested and rode the rest of the way back to Orbost. Percy Morris gave Julia some ground for a wedding present and they built a house there at Newmerella.

The Thomas family had eight daughters, Ethel was the youngest, and they had five sons. We used to go to see them—the Thorpes and the Peppers—and Ethel's brother Billy and me would go off to the river to listen to the old fellas talk. Sometimes there'd be a lot of us young blokes. The yarns they told and the names they called each other made us laugh.

Old Harry Stephen's son was Berty and everyone called him 'Narnge'. Nobody said Berty to 'im. Gee they were funny fellas, those. If you could only go back y'know. Old Narnge used to look around like that, just twist his head and all you could see was the big white balls of 'is eyes and we used to poke fun at him . . . if they'd known we was poking fun at them they'd 'ave half killed us. Narnge used to ride his bike to Orbost and camp there for a few days then go back to Lake Tyers. He had a little fox he'd stick in a bag and all you could see was this little nose stickin' out.

Berty's father was Harry Stephen, a full-blood, and he married Emily who had a white ancestor. The couple lived at Ramahyuck.

Emily and Harry had nine children (known of) and Berty was born about 1875. With the change of the Aboriginal Act in 1890, it was said Emily claimed her right as a 'half-caste' to be free and to earn a living off the station. In 1904 she took her children and left Ramahyuck to go hop-picking, but two weeks later she and Berty were so ill they had to be taken to the Sale Hospital where they remained for several months. Emily then asked permission to return to the station and she and her children were accepted back as residents.[1]

Ma and Pa Thomas (George and Agnus) with their granddaughter Mavis Stuart, 1926.

* See page 47.

George Thomas—we called him Pa Thomas—well he had some land surveyed, same as Billy Thorpe, and he got his bit of ground. He sold it a long time later and that land is where the new road to Orbost is now. Pa told us plenty of yarns too. When he was fencin' some of his land he told us how they did it when they were at Lake Tyers. They lined the fence up with the second button from the top on their shirts. 'Course if a fella was bigger or smaller he had to move up or down a button.

George and Billy always were great mates. If they were at a sports meeting they'd make a beeline for each other. They looked a bit alike too, both tall and with short pointed beards. Their first adventure with a piano when they were young fellas didn't stop them from buying a piano for their daughters. They had them taught and Ethel was a real good pianist.*

Ma and Pa Thomas taught their children how to get native food like swan-egging and the times and places to go, all that sort of thing. The girls learnt how to make the grass dilly-bags and Ma sold a lot she made for extra money to keep their large family. She went bean pickin' like most of the Aborigines then, they had to, there wasn't enough money about. They worked hard all their lives. Ma was a smart one and everyone knew her. A man just said to me the other day, 'Ma was a grand old lady and when it was bean time she'd be there.' She wouldn't let anyone put anything over her or cheek her—she'd be after them, she'd down anybody, and that's true . . . she even chased a friend of mine.

It was bean-pickin' season and Ma had knocked off for a cuppa tea, got the fire goin' and boiled her little billy. She just made the tea when along come this mate of mine and, as he was dying for a drink 'e thought he'd get on the right side of Ma, so he said real nicely, 'Dear old Ma, you shouldn't be workin' at the beans', and Ma said, 'Don't y'want me to earn any money?' He said, 'Aw you shouldn't be like that Ma. You oughta let your kids earn it.' Well, he said the wrong thing there, because those kids did work when they weren't at school. One thing led to another until Ma pulled a stick out of the fire and she chased him with it.

I saw that man years after and he told me about Ma chasing him with the fire-stick and what made Ma boil over in the finish was when she saw how much tea he wanted. He 'ad a rattling big buggy that he pulled out this pannikin from for Ma to fill with tea from her little billy, and he kept demanding the tea, so Ma up off after 'im and he didn't get the drink.

Ma and Pa told Ethel the Manaroo blacks used to be down at Newmerella in the early days, underneath the hill where the river was then. The tribe come down in their canoes on the main river. The river shifted with all the floods. In 1925 the Thomas family was caught in the floods at Orbost and they moved to higher ground then. The richest soil in Australia is there on the Newmerella flats. Sometimes there's so many cockatoos sitting on the willow trees there, they look like big white lilies in the branches.

When the electricity was connected at the new hall, Ethel's sister Julia was given the job of switching the first lights on. Those sisters were always giving each other frights and one night three of them, including Ethel, and meself were walking along the road in the dark and a rabbit shot across, throwing stones up as it went. Well, I don't know what them girls thought it was but they screamed and yelled and ran over to hang to me and they weren't so smart about giving each other frights after that.

One time while I was there, Simpson the policeman was looking for two

* Billy Thorpe's descendants presented his piano to the Bairnsdale museum.

(left to right) Back: **Ethel and Lucy Thomas.** Front: **Willie Murray and Dolly Thomas,** 1913.

dark men who were drunk and he wanted to lock 'em up for safety's sake but they got away from him and ran towards this house. Well, that policeman went round and round that place and couldn't find them. They'd hid themselves in the water tank—trouble was it was full and as they crouched down with their noses stuck up for air, the water slopped over the tank on to the ground and that's how Simpson caught them.

Pa told me when he was a young fella the old Snowy River ran all along the hillside and the young Aborigines in the tribe swam in the Snowy while the older men hunted possums. When they had enough *nullee* [meat] they waded along in the river and caught trout. There was plenty of blackfish, luderick, coming up from the salty water feeding along the river—perch and platypus too. The rivers and creeks were lousy with platypus in the early days, in fact Rev. Hagenauer got the Ramahyuck men to catch some for showing in Melbourne. There was salamander in that time too. I saw them years ago. They got a big hard head with big jaws and the nostril holes were about two or three inches across and the skin was that hard a pea rifle didn't hurt 'em. They was a sort of water lizard. They all disappeared along with the platypus after the 1934 floods.

Ethel's brothers worked hard and they saved enough between them to buy a car and that was the first car at Newmerella. They were good footballers and played for the team.

Toe holds cut in a tree, 1857 (The La Trobe Collection, State Library of Victoria).

Around about the 1920s the idea was to bring all the Aborigines to settle on Lake Tyers station and the people were brought from all over Victoria. It was about that time Grandfather and Granny Thorpe went back and Granny Conolly and her son Jack got permission to help them shift.

At a special meeting of the Board for the Protection of Aborigines in June 1917 it was resolved that all Aborigines, full-blood and 'half-caste', should be brought to the Lake Tyers station. This was the Concentration Plan. Lake Tyers was chosen because of its climatic conditions, lack of main roads and isolated position.

The Board decided to explain to the people if they were not willing to move to Lake Tyers they would forego the Board's assistance.

Under the Concentration Plan, made in the interests of economic management, the Aborigines who settled at Lake Tyers needed an adequate water supply and extra white staff to help manage the people and the station.

Thirty-six cottages were added at Lake Tyers and six more baths, and one of the cottages was fitted up as a hospital. In 1921 bores were put down for the necessary water supply to a depth of two hundred feet, without any result.

In 1923, the year Billy and Sarah Thorpe moved back to Lake Tyers, 230 survivors and descendants of the Victorian tribal groups had been brought together after six years of persistent effort, though some more Aborigines were still expected.* The first official count of the Victorian Aborigines in 1877 revealed a population of 293 part-Aboriginal persons and 774 full-blood Aborigines. There is no true figure established for the number of Aborigines at the time of white occupation of Victoria and estimates of the population made by the early squatters range from 3 000 to 17 000. Approximately 15 000 is believed to be the number of tribal people in 1834-5.[2]

Four generations at Lake Tyers. Kitty Johnson sitting. Behind her is Maggie (wife of Kitty's son, William, later known as Old Grandfather Johnson), Ada Harrison (neé Johnson) and her son.

Grandfather wasn't well enough to work, and he was gettin' on in years then, and when he took Sarah back to Tyers they had friends and relations on the station. Old Kitty Johnson, who'd rescued Billy and George after the last tribal fight, was still alive there and her son Billy was with her, but Larry her husband had died years before. Old Billy Thorpe's sister Eliza O'Rourke was there but o'course her husband Neddy was dead. Eliza's daughter Bella and her husband Johnny McDougall were on Tyers too. Then there was Henry Thorpe's widow, Julia and her husband Con Edwards and the Scotts, Bulls, McCreedies and lots more. So I s'pose Grandfather didn't mind going back; he always loved that place. They had the cottage nearest the lake, but that's not there now.

Where Grandfather and Granny Thorpe lived at Lakes Entrance there is a sign up now, 'Thorpes Lane'. You'd see it if you had a look. It's the signpost to the rubbish tip. Where Grandpa's house was is one of his plum trees still growing, and where Uncle Henry and Julia lived on the corner is a lily that Julia planted years ago and it still comes up every year.

There was any amount of work for the men on the station—clearing, fencing, ploughing and planting. In the earlier times one of the managers

Phillip at Thorpes Lane turn-off.

---

* Three years after Billy and Sarah moved to Lake Tyers, the transfer of the people of Aboriginal descent was complete. Eighty-eight full-bloods and three hundred and three part-Aborigines were receiving assistance from the Central Board for the Protection of Aborigines.

was showing the Aborigines how to sow seed, teaching them to farm, so he'd fill up pepper tins with seeds of Dutch and strawberry clover and give them to the men and say 'Go and throw it about the place.' That's what they did.

There was a time when someone thought there was oil to be found on the Tyers station and they bored for it out near the manager's house on top of the hill on the point. Grandfather Thorpe told us there were six or eight men had this triangle thing and they'd walk around so many times and then other men would take over and walk. If they'd gone down to Snuff Gully they might 'ave been luckier than they were on the point. Reggie Thorpe was out mustering cattle—he was only a young fella then about fifteen or sixteen—and he got off his horse to have a drink at Snuff Gully. He saw a little black rock and picked it up and it smelled like kerosene. He showed me the rock and if you lit that thing it burned. We never told about it, just kept it to ourselves, and no one would know where to look now.

After Rev. Bulmer died there was no minister, and if they'd allowed one things would have been better because the older people kept the young ones going to church. The people liked Frank Bulmer and they wanted him as the manager, but he wasn't. Bruce Ferguson was the manager when Billy Thorpe went back. There were some improvements on the station and one was the store for the Aborigines to buy from instead of them having to walk into Lakes Entrance. The men built a butcher's shop and it's still there in the township. 'Course, with all those Aborigines being brought to Tyers they got more white staff and some of those weren't liked by our people.

Some families were taken to Lake Tyers under an Order-in-Council—they were compelled to go. Once on the station the Aborigines could not leave without the written consent of the manager or Board and many objected to the authority held over them by the white staff, some of whom were not suited to their task. It was obvious to all how the Aborigines felt, as they asked to work outside the station; some would not obey orders; others left to visit their old home towns without permission.

The Board felt discipline and obedience was called for, and if the people did not co-operate with the staff a place of reform for the offenders was considered. After some discussion a Reformative Station for the people who did not behave or who committed some crime was suggested and Tortoise Head Island in Westernport Bay was named.[3]

They had footy and cricket on the station and some great matches were arranged, but they had to have permission to go off the station to play, and it got stopped after a while.

The tourists used to go to Lake Tyers. Blays had a boarding house on the hill and they had a boat to take their guests over the lake to the settlement. Eliza O'Rourke's son Jimmy was a guide for the white visitors and her daughter Bella's husband Johnny McDougall was a guide too.

The Aborigines would put on a turn—a concert—for the tourists and they'd have the Fire Makers and the Boomerang Throwers demonstrating. There'd be boat-loads of people come over to the settlement for this. One time there was an accident when some of the tourists were going round the lake in a motor launch. It caught fire and the people rushing about tipped it, and two young girls from the station saw what happened and they jumped into a boat and rowed out to the people. They brought as many as they could the first time and then returned and got some more. There was one man they

79

couldn't save. He was caught under the boat; he was the store-keeper from Lake Tyers. When they got all the people back on shore, one of the girls said, 'I'll go and ring the police.' Now one of the women who was rescued by the girls reckoned she wouldn't know how to use a telephone or even know how to go about telling someone what happened. Someone else who had been saved by these two girls said, 'That Aboriginal girl wasn't too dumb to go out and save you.'

Con Edwards was a guide too and these fellas took the visitors round the place for them to buy boomerangs and baskets and all sorts of things the Aborigines made for sale.

Billy Thorpe's and George Thomas's long-time friend, old Kitty Johnson, was the oldest on the station and the white people always wanted to see her. She made a lot of money for her grandchildren from the tourists; she wouldn't spend it on herself. One Christmas I was out there when the tourists were all about taking photos of the Aborigines on the station. Old Granny Johnson always wore a scarf over her head and smoked a clay pipe; well Connie Edwards said he'd take some of the tourists to see this real old lady—she knew the old language—well, when they got to her house there she was sittin' out the front with her head covered with a possum-skin rug, and she wouldn't pull her head out from it. She sat there listening to the tourists askin' her to let 'em see her so they could get a photo, but she just sat there. After a good bit of coaxing all of a sudden she shoved 'er hand out and stuck a mug on the ground in front of her and she waited till she reckoned there was enough coins dropped in, then she pulled the rug off and sat there grinnin' away, smokin' her pipe for the tourists to photograph her. The whites often gave her tobacco and before they left she'd bring out some boomerangs and some baskets she made herself. They'd last ten years y'know, and she got ten shillings for them. Sometimes the little kids had nicked spears from their fathers and gave them to Granny to sell for them.

There was the time when Andrew Chase got hold of some wine and he and the old girl got drunk on it and the police tried to take old Granny to gaol—for her own safety they said. Andrew was about fifteen stone and well-spoken but he couldn't talk the policeman out of taking Granny so he pushed him over. The policeman tried to explain Granny wouldn't be locked in the cell and she could come out when she liked, but Andrew hit him and they had to go to court over this. Well, the people worded Granny up about what to say in court when they asked 'er about the wine, and they told her to say 'I got it from this fella behind me.' Granny practised that till the day they went to court. Well, all her relations and friends went to court too, Grandfather Thorpe and me Dad Percy went, and when the magistrate said to her, 'Do you know the meaning of an oath?' Old Granny Johnson looked at him, gave a grin and nodded her head and said, 'Yair boss, I get it from this fella behind me here.' Everybody in the place laughed and the magistrate said to old Kitty, 'You had better go. You do not know the meaning of an oath.'

Every now and again the tourists were stopped by the Government and managers from goin' to Lake Tyers station and that gave the people less money for extra food. I come up from Koo-wee-rup one time there for a few days to see Grandfather Thorpe when he had a work contract to do some fencin' on the station. He had Granny Thorpe with 'im and they were all right for tukka but a lot of the others weren't. They got their rations that had to last a week.

Lake Tyers Station in the 1920s.

I was out there one day when Albert Lind* was there and Old Granny Kitty Johnson called him over and give him a look at the bread ration she had—two little loaves to last the week. She also got one cup of sugar, three cups of flour, half a cup of tea and that was her supply for a week, with a bit of meat. She told Lind it wasn't enough to live on and she was too old then to hunt, but she was a good fisherman so she got extra that way. Anyway Lind got other members of the Protection Board, and he thrashed 'em for giving such a small amount of food for the people to live on and said they took the country from these people and put them there at the lake and this is the way we treat them. He said, 'We should be ashamed of ourselves. Why can't we give 'em more rations, double up on the meat.' He told the manager Old Kitty had to have extra food and a fresh loaf of bread every second day instead of having stale bread for a week.

When that old lady died in 1924 she must have been a hundred. No one knew how old she was. It didn't seem to be much longer after she died that one of the little boys she reared up when she found him also died—my grandfather Billy Thorpe.

Then when we saw the Dad, it was his turn to tell us about the early days . . . how Henry Thorpe played footy with Lakes Entrance and, when his side was getting beat, he'd take off his boots and play in bare feet. He was a high jumper and he'd go head and shoulder over the players and mark over the top of 'em . . . The games Dad played with Stratford with Haines Cameron,

* Albert Lind represented the East Gippsland electorate in the Legislative Assembly from October 1920 to June 1961 and he was a Shire Councillor for thirteen years. He was knighted in 1951.

81

Donald's son . . . When the gold was about and sheep come from the gold-bearing places, they often had gold stuck in their teeth from nibbling the grass down low after wet weather, when the gold had been knocked into the grass . . . And Billy Barlow, whenever his wife wanted to go to Sydney Billy Barlow would swim the river and get in a cave and take gold from the rocks. He'd sell it to the publican and that would pay for their trip to Sydney and Billy never showed anybody where 'e got it from and they called it Billy Barlow's Gold Mine . . . When horses for India was in great demand and Jack and Ted Mullett got sent to India to look after some of the horses . . . One story was how Granny, Dad's mother, told them stories about a big blackfella they called Big Charlie. I've seen a photo Granny had of him and his mate Short Harry, the one that got the *nargun*.

Well, Big Charlie and this little short fat fella Harry travelled between Ramahyuck and Lake Tyers after the people got settled in at those two stations. Big Charlie was a shearer for the settlers and he was paid with sovereigns in those days, and when he died Granny found ten or twelve of those sovereigns in his pocket and she sewed them into his waistcoat and buttoned it up and said nothing to any person about it. Nobody knew and Big Charlie got buried with his sovereigns. Years later Granny told the Dad and Walter McCreedie and Herb Murray; well those three blokes had great fun teasin' poor old Granny. They reckoned they was gonna dig up Big Charlie and get his sovereigns and they'd say, 'Come on Granny, tell us where he is', and the Dad would say to her, 'Go on Ma, tell us', but of course Granny never told. Those sovereigns belonged to Big Charlie and they still do.

When Granny Louise Conolly and Granny Sarah Thorpe were both widows, they lived together at Bairnsdale with Granny Conolly's son Jack and his wife Allie, who was Granny Thorpe's daughter. Granny Thorpe died first, then Granny Conolly lived with her daughter Emily and husband Dick Chapman. After that Granny went back to Jack and Allie until she died in the 1930s. She was a real old lady then. Granny Conolly was buried in the double grave with Granny Thorpe in the old Bairnsdale cemetery.

I was asked by a white man once how our people buried the dead in the early days. He said, 'I suppose they had to use a stick to dig the holes.'

I told him, 'Have you seen how the wombats dig a long burrow?' Our people took advantage of this. They tied a piece of bark around under the armpits and with a long forked stick, without scarring the body, would push that body into the burrow as far as they wanted. Sometimes they used sticks to widen or deepen the burrow. When the rain comes this burrow fills in and in years to come the silt builds up around the opening. They used old trees, too, by scooping the inside out of it and the dead were put in there. Other times a breakaway in the ground was used and three or four could be put in. This is what my grandmother and grandfather told me and also the wife's father told me back in 1936—and they seen the people buried in this way.

These old native grounds and burial places shouldn't be disturbed or dug up. Not long ago some white men wanted to dig up some Aborigines' graves and we told them if they wanted to dig up old graves to start on the Melbourne Cemetery—dig up some of those old graves first, and if the white people allowed it they could start on ours then. I said to one of these men, 'Why do you want to dig up our peoples' bones? Let them lie there to rest; they were put there to rest, let them stay there.' Now there's some talk about them putting our peoples' bones in tin cans and plantin' them somewhere else.

CHAPTER TEN

Managers at Lake Tyers

THERE NEVER WAS ANOTHER MANAGER ON THE MISSION LIKE JOHN BULMER. A few years after John Bulmer was made a minister of the Church of England the government took the station over, and that was the finish of it being called a mission. They must have thought Rev. John Bulmer was getting old and needed help because they sent in a bloke called Captain Howe. He was a hard man, that one. He was the manager then, not John Bulmer. John stayed on in his home there with his wife. He looked after the religious side of the business. He died in 1913 at eighty years of age and is buried at the Lakes Entrance cemetery, not far from Rachel Thorpe. She died eight years before Rev. Bulmer when she was twenty-three.

It's got on his gravestone, John Bulmer was a devoted worker amongst the Aborigines, and that's true. He was a friend to the people and everyone who knew him said he was a great man—a good man. Mrs Bulmer died five years after him.

After Captain Howe left, Bruce Ferguson was the manager and the Aborigines had the vegetable gardens goin' so good the people could buy the vegies as well as grow them. He had good crops of beans too; anyway he was getting on in years, probably about in his sixties, when he left the station in 1924, and the residents kept on growing a few beans and lookin' after the ground.

The next manager was a bloke named Baldwin and he was good on the farm and worked in with the men. Eliza O'Rourke was a grandmother by then and she give us a lot of the news. Not only Granny Thorpe told us—she was there too—but we knew all the people on the station.

Well, the beans did so well the men wanted to sell 'em outside and they got two or three hundred pounds one time, but that brought trouble from the local farmers. They reckoned they was competing with the Aborigines and they told the local Member for Parliament, Mr Lind—he wasn't a Sir then—and he took their side and told the Board for Protection of the Aborigines that a number, I don't know how many there were, objected to Lake Tyers marketing beans. Y'see, the truth was they lost their cheap labour when the Aborigines wanted to grow their own and instead of workin' for them they was workin' for themselves.

Baldwin stuck up for the Tyers blokes but he couldn't win and they stopped them selling the beans. They wanted to catch and sell the fish too and that was stopped. That was a pity, because workin' like that showed them they could make something out of themselves, 'ave a future for their families, something to aim for. Anyway that was that; they got stopped.

Baldwin didn't stay there long and the next man they had in charge of the station and the people was Captain Newman. Now Captain Newman was a beauty, he loved the people and they loved and respected him. See, respect is important and a lot of those whites who were in charge of the Aborigines there or who worked there, white women too, the people had no respect for them . . . for very good reasons. The Aborigines knew what some of those whites in charge were like.

Captain Newman had a good know-how about farmin' before he was a sailor—and sailing around Australia give him knowledge about our people, the way they lived and their medicines. He understood the Aborigines, he did everything to keep them healthy, he saved lives out there on the station. When Alfie Carter, Charlie's father, was sick, he told the people to fill up a cart with eucalyptus leaves and bring it to him. He chucked them on a fire and while they was smokin' he threw a blanket over them, got Alfie to lay on that and, with another blanket over the top of Alfie, he put more leaves around. The steam come through and it wasn't long before Alfie was well again.

He used another of our mixtures for bad pain, like the pain y'get from cancer. We still use it for our people. You get a weed we call pink weed and boil all of it up, leaves and everything, and take it like a medicine. Another one is to get the root of a fern, peel off the brown skin, cover and boil it up. You can use goanna oil for gout. We used the milk from thistles to bring boils to a head.

One time my wife Ethel's eyes were crook and the doctor said she had cataracts and sent her to a hospital in Melbourne, and when she got there she sat and waited and waited and no one come to her to see what was wrong, so she got sick of that and come home again. We went to see Captain Newman and he give her some ointment to put in the eyes and that cured the cataracts. He was a real herbalist, that man. He was on the right track, using the natural cures from the ground like the herbs. Our people had to do it and they knew what plants and roots, berries and juices were safe to use, and what to use them for too. Ethel used to collect herbs for him and the small box gums with the roots intact too. He used 'em all.

White people might think our medicine men were a bit *denbin-n-th-brook* when I tell you what they did to make sick people better. *Denbin-n-th-brook?* That's our language for 'gone in the head'. Now my own mother told me this story I am going to tell you. She saw it happen when she was a young girl.

One time Gordon O'Rourke, Neddy and Eliza's boy, had a crook side, see? It was giving him some terrible pain, so the old people got their own doctor to come to him. Well, he gathered up some rib-grass and other herbs and he plonked it all on Gordon's side where the pain was, then he stuck a reed in Gordon's mouth and started blowin'. After a bit he poked and prodded Gordon, talkin' and mumblin' all the time in his old language. After a while the sore part started to swell up like a boil and, after about an hour of all this business, the medicine man squeezed Gordon's side and out shot a bone. Gordon was as healthy as anyone after that—cured.

I don't reckon any of us would like to be stitched up the way the old tribal people did the job and I saw this done. An old *gunai* had this big cut on his arm—I can't remember how it happened but the old fellas closed it up for 'im. You ever seen those long red bull-dog ants? They bite into the flesh and do they sting. Well, the old fellas found an ant-bed and, quick as a flash, the old bloke who was doin' the stitchin' picks up a bull-dog with the tips of his fingers, holds the sides of the wound tight together and puts the bull-dog on. The bull-dog bites into the skin, and the doctorin' bloke nipped its head off,

Special leaves, grasses and pink weed used for 'Pink Weed Cure'.

84

so there was stitch number one. Then he got another, stuck it on and, as soon as the bull-ant bit, off with 'is head. Right up that *gunai*'s arm that medicine man went. You might think that was a cruel thing to do to those bull-dogs, but that poor bloke must've suffered. One bite is enough. Anyway, 'e was stitched up.

The old porcupines love eating bull-dog ants, just lolls his tongue out along the ground and the ants walk on to it and that's the end of them.

I can remember when Otto Login's* wife Alice had a bad time with her legs. They were going paralysed and Otto used to fill two kero tins with sea water and heat it up and Alice put her feet in. They had these things they wind to get electricity and they'd stick it in the water, vibrating it see? Made her legs all tingly like electric shocks. Otto did that three times a day and Alice got the use of her legs again. I couldn't have been very old then but I can see them now, getting bags and a rubber seat ready for Alice to sit on for the treatment.

When I told a doctor once about our Aboriginal cures he just said there were enough drugs about now to use, and he wasn't interested. Captain Newman knew better all those years ago.

Captain Newman told the people when there was any troubles or problems on the station to get together and talk it out and decide what had to be done themselves if anyone had done something they shouldn't. Something like what John Bulmer had going in the real early days of the mission.

There was a lot of sickness amongst the people while Newman was there and they had to often go to the Bairnsdale Hospital for X-rays. He had a little hospital on the station where two of the girls, Winnie Murray and the girl Johnson, helped him with nursing, but when the people were bad they had to go to Bairnsdale. The hospital needed an X-ray unit and Captain Newman hit on an idea to raise money to help, and because a lot of our people went there, everyone at Tyers was willing to work in with 'im. They got their concert group on the go, playing the gum-leaf and dancing and singing, and Captain Newman took those people travellin' round, into New South too, and they raised money for that equipment for the hospital at Bairnsdale to show their appreciation for what the hospital did for them.

Tourists still went to the station and old Kitty Johnson's son by then was a grandfather himself and he made boomerangs that all the whites wanted to buy. He was a good gardener on the vegetables too. When the tourist season was coming, him and a lot of the men hunted around for the best wattle trees to get the root for the boomerangs. They cut the root right through and used the rasp to turn the boomerang and sometimes they'd mark it with hot irons or wire.

When Captain Newman left, new rules come in and the tourists didn't come so often. He was only at Tyers for a couple of years I think, but our people kept going to see him where he lived. He had a lime works at Tooloo Arm and a few of the Aborigines got work with him. A lot of our sick people got treated by him there. They crossed the lake from the settlement to get his medicine; the Aborigines trusted him and liked him so much. Captain Newman was a good man but we never knew why he left the station. My wife Ethel's sister's husband Herb Murray was one who worked for him at the lime works.

Lake Tyers was under Captain Newman's management from 1929–31 and

* Otto Login: born 1869, died 1917. He was Braggin Scott's step-brother.

85

(left to right) Foster Moffatt playing the gum leaf, Con Edwards, Les 'Bully' Green, Jack Conolly (Phillips uncle), Rev. Douglas Nicholls (Sir Douglas), Alice (Phillip's aunt) playing the piano, and another vocalist, Bessy Moffatt.

in those two years he appears to have gained more friendship and respect from the Aborigines than any of the managers, apart from Rev. John Bulmer. Lake Tyers had twelve managers from 1861 to 1968, when the position was terminated.

It was almost impossible for any of the Aborigines who had left the station to find any work during the depression years and several went to Captain Newman for work. By 1933 he was employing eight men who had been under his charge at Lake Tyers.

The likely reason for Captain Newman's leaving Lake Tyers was that he displeased the Board because, in trying to help the residents, he allowed some of the families to 'run up' accounts.[1]

VISITING LAKE TYERS

Sometimes at Christmas we went to the lake to camp and we'd go over to the settlement in a boat during the day. There was a place near an area where the old people always said there was a ghost hung round in the scrub—y'could see it from one side of the lake. Auntie Julia's place was near one of the arms of the lake and one night Ethel and Julia and one or two others went down to Lakes Entrance to meet the boat from Bairnsdale and it was late at night, about nine o'clock. To get back to Julia's place it was just a track through the bush, and they were making their way along and Julia said, 'Hurry up,' so everybody hurried. Julia was puffing and pantin' but just the same she said to hurry up faster, so everybody got moving real fast along that old foot track. They were all scootin' along down the hill towards the lake where the boat was and Julia hollers out, 'Keep hurryin,' and by then everyone's pantin' and puffin'. They got to the boat and pushed it out so hard it nearly reached the other side of the lake and landed in the ti-tree. 'Course, they all wanted to know why they had to hurry and Julia told them, 'There was someone hangin' on me back coming down to the boat—it just kept holdin' on.'

Auntie Julia had a bag on her shoulder with all her little parcels in it and whatever it was, or whoever, it just hung on tight, but there wasn't nothing on it in the boat. Ethel said she'd never walk down there again at night . . . and she never has again.

Granny Eliza O'Rourke used to cross the lake from the settlement at a different place, near Blays Hill. She went over every morning in the holiday times, and cooked fish the old way for the tourists—plaster the fish with mud and cook it in the hot sand like they did the damper, and if the tourists had any spuds she tossed 'em in the ashes for them. The white people loved it and they picnicked there near the old mahogany tree that was covered with creeper and looked beautiful in the spring. The maggies and wattle-birds built in it. The houses block off everything now and some places you can't see the mission church on the hill at the settlement. There were a few old fishermen around here; Charlie Cross and Peter Brett were two, white fellas they were. They netted on the lake and they had a water tank to tan the nets in so the fish couldn't see them. They stuck wattle-bark in the water to brown up the nets and then they left 'em to dry on some racks.

Depression Days

PHILLIP PEPPER MARRIES ETHEL THOMAS

Eileen, 'Jumbo' and Les, with Nipper the family dog.

OUT OF WORK

Eileen, aged seven years.

ETHEL THOMAS KNEW ME FOR YEARS BEFORE WE MARRIED. OUR FAMILIES always mixed together—the Thomas kids and the Peppers and Thorpes all grew up together, and after our family left the swamp farm at Koo-wee-rup I had to travel round for work like plenty of other young dark and white blokes me own age. Anyway I got work cuttin' timber. Ride the bike I did to the different places until Ma Thomas, Ethel's mother, told me I could stay at their place at Newmerella. Well Ethel and me got keen on each other and we decided to get married and after I got the Thomas's approval—Ma said, 'Why not? We've known you a long time Phil, and we know you can provide for Ethel'—so we had a quiet wedding, nothing flash. That was in 1928. None of us had money to spare to invite all Orbost but we had a nice little reception at Ma's after. No honeymoon though, we couldn't afford that because we didn't want to risk our jobs by takin' time off for honeymoonin' so it was back to work the next day.

Some people didn't even know we were married for a while. Ethel's boss said to her, 'I believe Phil Pepper got married, Ethel. Who's the girl?' Didn't she have a laugh. That was Jack Irvine, a real good bloke. Ethel and her mum both went to Irvines to do the washing and housework for 'em and when she wasn't there Ethel had days at the dentist and down at another farm, too, riding her horse round to these places. We lived with Ma and Pa Thomas for a while.

Well things started to get tougher soon after we married, because the Depression was gettin' on us, sneakin' in. By the time we had three little ones, Les, Eileen and Jumbo, work was hard to find and I did any sort of job to keep goin'. We got two bob a bag to pick beans then, but things got worse, and Ma said go and see that fella Albert Lind. I did. I asked him, could he get a licence for me to go and cut timber, but he said, 'Phil, you can't get into the bush at this time but if you'd like to go on the dole—what we plan now for the people—and you're willin' to work while you're on it, I'll see what I can do. No good givin' money for nothin' to the people and I can't make a bludger out of you, Phil. If you're prepared to work for your bread and butter for a month, you'll hear from me when the month is up.'

Sure enough I did get a letter from him, one day before the month was up. For that month, while I waited for the time to pass he said to work on the dole, I worked around the shire on the roads, cleaning up drains, levelling off and all that. There were three hundred of us there on what we'll call the dole and there were six Aboriginal boys working amongst 'em. We got no money for three and a half days a week of work, but we did get a piece of paper, a voucher, for food, see? Worth seventeen shillin's and sixpence. But we was cunnin'! We worked the full week all the time—the shire let us—and then if it was wet or somethin' happened one week and we couldn't work, we still got the voucher.

J. W. McLachlan, speaking in the Legislative Assembly, said there were 80,000 men, women and children in Victoria dependent upon sustenance, and these were only the registered persons, as there must be at least another 20,000 not registered who were dependent on sustenance.[1]

Now this letter from Lind told me I could get three months work and that would take me into the bean pickin' season, and he said if I still wanted to go into the timber in the next year, he would fix it up for me. When I left off the dole work I had a week owing to me but I didn't worry about that. I was too happy to get work in the forestry and I worked there till Jack Irvine gave me work on his farm ploughin', getting eight bob a day, and that meant I was home more with Ethel and the kids. I rode me bike to his place until he gave us a little place on the farm. The three children went to school at Newmerella.

When the work finished at Jack's farm I took the family to Koo-wee-rup and I was diggin' spuds, forty bags a day, for Dick O'Hare, and we lived in a returned soldier's house. We had to move from the house to a shed on higher ground when we got flooded. I picked maize for the Frenchy over the road too and the boys and Eileene went to a local school at Cardinia Swamp.

Ethel and Eileen.

One of our old neighbours at Dad's farm left there before I took my family back. They were Jack and Hilda Dixon and they bought the house and land where the Police Paddocks are at Rowville near Dandenong. That's where the Native Police and the Ned Kelly trackers were quartered in the real early days and the Dixons lived in the house that was built in the 1840s for the bloke in charge.* We used to ride our horses from Dad's farm to see them there. I went to see that place lately, the first time me feet has been on that ground in fifty years.

On the weekends at Koo-wee-rup, we took spuds down to our friends and relations to help them along down in Melbourne, where they shifted, chasing work, and when my work finished on the swamp they said come down there and get work and they would put us up, so we did. I got work at Millers rope works on the night shift because Ethel worked at Leggos factory in the day and that way there was always one of us with the kids when they got home from school.

After a while we got word that Ethel's father was very sick. He died and we went back home to Orbost to Ma Thomas and, after she was all right again, we bought a house on the highway at Newmerella and I worked for Jimmy Nixon and stopped with him for about twenty-seven years. If Peter or Toby Nixon wanted anything done Jimmy would send me over there and I filled in the slack times this way. It meant I didn't have to leave me family either because I just crossed the river in me own boat or rode the bike to nearer places when Jimmy didn't need me on his farm.

There was a good white fella Ethel worked for. He was a bank manager and she did the cleaning in the bank and anything left on the floor she'd just pick it up and put it in its place. There'd be money there too. Ethel will tell about that.

Eileen and Phillip in Melbourne.

'Oh, I'd start off in the Bank at the front first, cleaning all that up. The

* Henry Pulteney Dana, Commandant of the Native Police Corps. Pulteney Street Dandenong is named after him.

money would be laying everywhere, I'd just push it aside, all in a heap and clean up. He'd come in after and I'd have everything cleaned up and polished out before they opened up. From there I'd go right on out to the kitchen and finish up with the washing. I'd get two days a week working there, sometimes I got nearly a week at a time. After work, they'd take me home, driving me to Marlo first, just for the outing. That bank manager and his wife were real nice folk. When they left, they wanted me to go too and he said he would get work for Phillip but he wouldn't leave Jimmy Nixon. I visited them at Dandenong and we had a good old yarn then.'

That's true. Jimmy was havin' a bad time too. And I worked a lot for the Irvines on their maize and beans in between times with Jimmy. We had trouble sometimes with what we called candle-grease-speck on the beans. One paddock of beans could get infected, then it'd be spread to a good paddock by foxes and birds. You'd see the little larks come—the little devils would be up in the air whistling away happy, then they'd get tired o' that and come down and roll around in the bean bushes, little feathers touching the good bushes, then they'd fly away as sparky as could be, off to someone else's paddock to spread the disease. I saw a fox take a chook off across the beans and when it come time to pick you could see the line of the infection. Foxes aren't satisfied with one track. They criss-cross the paddocks and that's the end of that paddock of beans.

When the bean-picking seasons were on during the 1930s a lot of the fellas from Lake Tyers station come to Orbost for the pick—women and children

Beans loaded ready to thresh, Snowy River flats.

Leslie, Phillip and Ethel's grand-daughter, holds a basket made by Bella Cameron with native grass.

sometimes too, and they'd camp around for the season. Other times they were brought up in the truck and taken back if they were day jobs; they got the pass for that from the manager. They had to have a pass. Some of the men had permission for different times. Others went maize or bean and pea pickin' without the permit from the manager and they copped it. Sometimes their rations were stopped or they got fined a couple quid—a lotta money then. They were usually allowed to go home to the station after a while. Permission from the manager was the important thing for those people.

When I was working at Toby Nixon's some of the Tyers men were there and, by gee, some of those fellas were good pickers, they were getting three bob a bag and they could pick their ten or fifteen bags a day. They'd buy food and new clothes for their kids and go home to Tyers with a pocketful of money and those managers didn't know just how much money they did have. Other times, later on, they worked at young Peter's usually by day, come up in the truck, and Peter Nixon threw in their dinner as well and some meat. Mrs Nixon would have cakes for the children and they'd take some of all this back home to Tyers at night. An old Aboriginal woman there at Nixons was Bella Cameron, Eiza Thorpe and Neddy O'Rourke's daughter. She was Johnny McDougall's widow and was married to Haines Cameron, Donald's son . . . well Bella used to cook the meat and get it all ready to give to the people, the workers from Tyers, not us who was workin' there all the time, and Bella would give the tukka out to 'em. See, these blokes from Tyers were full-bloods and not allowed off the Lake Tyers station then.

Sometimes the blokes working for Nixons stayed overnight on the farm and then someone would come down with a can of milk and a drum of tea for us. They were always good to the dark people.

CRICKET AND FOOTBALL AT TYERS

The Lake Tyers mob could play cricket and footy as good as they picked the beans. Major Glen was the manager at Tyers in the thirties and forties and he got the permission for them to play outside the station in the East Gippsland matches. He was the first man that started a team with a coach from Melbourne; Drummond was his name. He didn't 'ave to coach Reggie Thorpe though, he knew all the tricks, and Con Edwards and Charlie Green, they knew more than Drummond ever learnt. Reggie could kick a football from a standing kick, a stab kick, he was a wizard on that. They won the East Gippsland premiership in 1934 and they pulled off the cricket premiership that same year. The premiership was at Orbost and a bloke at the bottom pub, Harry Gardiner, had a hundred pounds on 'em. Well the crowd reckoned Tyers was done at half-time and they started leaving the ground and goin' to the pub, and by three-quarter time they was sure the Lake Tyers team had lost. Well, they played Reggie in the back line, so as soon as the ball went down they changed over and Reggie come in and he said to Bob Andy and Jack McCleod, 'You pass it to me and I'll take it on the run,' and, bang bang, he kicked ten goals straight and they won it by a point by changing Thorpy to the front. When they come off the ground Harry Gardiner wanted to know who won and when they told him he pushed all the white people out of the bar and said, 'There y'are boys, drink yer heads off.' They did and they got into trouble for it, but they enjoyed themselves first.

The Lake Tyers men had another go in 1938 and they won the premiership then too.

Lake Tyers belonged to the East Gippsland League and the team was referred

The Concert Group: *(left to right) Back:* Laurie 'Dodge' Moffatt, 'Chook' Mullett, Tom Foster, Herb Murray, Con Edwards, Bob Andy, Lance McDougall. *Front:* Jimmy Scott, Winnie Murray, Delia Murray, Nugget Harrison, ____Faye, Nora Foster, _____, Bertha Green, Frank Wandin, 1920s.

to as 'the fleet footed men of Lake Tyers'. They had the reputation for 'running its opponents off their legs'.[2]

THE RED BUFFS FOOTBALL TEAM

The station had a sports fund and they raised money for the equipment and the trips away by having concerts and things, but sometimes when some of the kids were sick, or away from their home on the station, the sports fund money had to be used to pay fares for the parents to go and see them.

During the Depression time we had a football team called the Red Buffs, made up of white fellas and Aboriginal boys—the Aborigines were the best players. Old Lance Ashby was a bit of a character and he 'ad a dog that he swore would do everything he told him, the dog always tagged along with Lance. Anyway, we always were stuck for somewhere to have our meetings and we'd get in the bush near the Newmerella Hall there, make a fire and have our yarns, and hold the meeting. One night we was all talkin' about the training and Herb Murray said, 'I reckon we oughta go out and get a goanna, get the fat outta him and mix it up with the metho and eucalyptus—it'll make a real good rub.' Old Joe, a sleeper-cutter, was there and he said he knew where there was a goanna, he'd seen it out where he was cuttin', so the next day Herb Murray got his spring-cart and harnessed up 'is horse in it and we was ready to go.

Lance took his dog and reckoned he knew how to catch that goanna . . . they can be nasty y'know, they'll fight with their teeth and claws and whack you with the tail if they get a chance. Some of the fellas went in the spring-cart and Billy Thomas, Ethel's brother, and me, we rode our bikes, and when we got there here's this stump about seven feet high and Joe said the goanna was inside. A few bashes on the stump and it scurried to the top and poked its head out, so Lance got his axe; he thought he'd thump 'im on the head and knock 'im out. He was standing in the cart, see, and he took a swing at the goanna and knocked the inside of the stump and the goanna jumped out and

92

raced up a stringy-bark saplin' and it gave the horse and Lance such a fright the horse jumped and Lance fell out of the cart.

Well, 'e up and after that goanna up the tree. 'Course the saplin' shook as Lance got up and the further he climbed, the goanna went higher, till there was no tree left hardly. One more shake and the goanna fell right out of the branches on to the ground. 'Get it, boy', he yells out to 'is dog, sooling him on to it, and the dog turned 'im back. Next minute the goanna heads straight back up the tree and Lance is there hangin' on, hollerin' 'Get some sticks and poke 'im off, get 'im down outta here,' but we couldn't, we was all rollin' round laughin' at Lance.

The goanna shot across 'is back, diggin' the claws in as 'e went, and Lance tried to lean away from it, but instead he fell out of the tree—he was up there about twelve or fifteen feet—The goanna come too and belted off into the stump and everybody left it there. That was the end of the goanna fat.

CYCLE RACING

We did a lot of bike riding in those days and I was in the first race from Sale to Melbourne. It was a terrible crook day, rainin' and hail all the time, and on the return leg about twelve of us got as far as Pakenham, dead beat. I said, 'I'm going on the milk train, boys,' and we all ended up on the milk train and we got home before the rest of the riders. They all reckoned we was pretty good cyclists.

It wasn't all fun in them times, we worked for our crust during the Depression years. Albert Lind got work for the people during the Depression and the blacks and whites worked side be side. Lind was a good politician. If you asked him something, he'd tell you. Now if you ask anything, they say, 'We'll look into it,' and they're still lookin' twelve months later.

ABORIGINES IN THE DEPRESSION

Our people who didn't have houses during that time, who camped, well their friends that had any food helped them. Sometimes they camped near the Lake Tyers Station, not on it—they weren't allowed—and someone would get food to them. See, we had men and women from New South Wales married to our people, but the trouble was the laws for the Aborigines were different, and if they'd lived for a time at Walligah Lake reserve or somewhere else, then come to Gippsland, the authorities said go back over the border. And it was the same over there. They'd say, you been living in Victoria, go back there. So what could they do? They camped in the bush or in the parks. They had a law in New South Wales that said the dark people couldn't live within so many miles of an Aboriginal reserve; so the ones who belonged to Gippsland brought their families back here.

At Lake Tyers they had an idea for keeping people who did not belong away from the place. I know a Christian bloke who went there to visit and he was told to stand outside the gate. Well they swore in about four blackfellas on the station as special constables. Jack Macleod was one and old Ted Mullett too, and they had to go around and see there were no white fellas or 'Aboriginal outsiders' on the station. That's right. All the girls and boys belonging on the station had to be in at a certain time.

The powers of the Aborigines Protection Board were published by the Bairnsdale Advertiser *early in 1934. At that time the nominal chairman of the Board was the Chief Secretary and the vice-chairman was the Under Secretary; an explanation by the Board regarding the decision made some years earlier to close the reserves and place the Aborigines on the Lake Tyers station revealed that about eight elderly Aborigines were still at Framlingham, near Warrnambool. The group had been allowed to live there 'for sentimental reasons which included the fact they had relations buried there'. The position at Lake Tyers in respect to assistance for any descendants of the Victorian tribal Aborigines either living on the Lake Tyers station or living outside the station, was that those people 'defined as quadroons or octoroons could not receive assistance from the Board'. The Aboriginal Protection Act gave the Board no power for this aid to be made possible.[3]*

The work that Captain Newman gave the Aborigines during the Depression come in handy for them and their families, but if you had to get the dole you worked for it, making roads, carting stones, chippin' grass, all sorts of jobs, and you were better for it, none of this bludgin' on the government and others. Nowdays some get their cheque and cross the border and get another; there oughta be a bit of work around for 'em to do.

During those bad times the churches had collections of clothes for the poor people and I've seen young girls gettin' big dresses, turning 'em inside out and sewing 'em together again for beautiful dresses for themselves. All the white people too were happy to get these clothes. They didn't have enough money to buy clothes with either, then, y'know. We could all go to the different churches to pick out clothes and if anything didn't fit we swapped it around with someone else's.

I knew a bloke real well named Frank Pollard, a car salesman he was. He sold the Thomas boys a Chev. in 1926—they picked it out of the bean paddock at sixpence a bag and it cost them one hundred and twenty pounds. Well, one day, up the street some of us doleys was talkin' and jokin' with one another when we saw Frank Pollard comin' up and he said to me, 'Well how are you goin', Phil?' and I told him I was O.K. I looked down at me boots what I had wired up to keep the sole on and he must've noticed that because he told me to go round to his place after. Well that man gave me a beautiful suit and some pointy toed shoes, and when I wore them all me doley mates used to joke at me, and they nicknamed me Frank Pollard and said I should be goin' round selling cars. We had a sense of humour that kept us all going. When things come good years after, we bought a car from Frank. He lived till he was the ripe old age of ninety and he was a wonderful person. He wouldn't walk past anyone he knew. Always had a word for them. He thought a lot of Ma Thomas and her family.

All the fellas liked to have a cigarette but of course we couldn't afford many, so when we rolled a smoke we'd only have half of it and keep the other half for next time.

On the whole, the majority of the Aborigines that I've known have appreciated what they had, and they were always happy with very little. They would share and share alike among themselves. If they've got anything and you haven't got it the majority of people would say, 'Look, you better have half of this.' The poor whites were the same too, and in the Depression years when I had a good garden goin' of me own, I'd take pumpkins or other vegetables to poor whites, and when I didn't have anything goin' they'd share with us what they had. Poor whites were no different to the poor dark people.

A lot of city men come to the country lookin' for work in the Depression. Sometimes they made a go of it picking with the farmers like Ethel and me, and some of the Aborigines who lived in Gippsland. One time we were going out to Jimmy Nixon's for the beans in his truck and out near Dinner Creek she yells out to Jimmy, 'Hey Jim, there's two ducks in that little water-hole there', and Jim stopped the truck, grabbed his gun and sneaked back—sang out—the ducks flew out and he got the pair of 'em. Ethel's cataracts were cured all right.

The 1934 floods brought the Deddick down and left it all over the Snowy River and we got a lot of Murray pine that come down; it had a lovely scenty smell. When any of the floods were on, the people used to come out and stand on the hill at Newmerella to watch the flats get flooded. In the 1934 floods the water was up to two boards off the top of the houses and the people sat on the roofs waiting to be collected by boat. From the top of the hill we could see Toby Nixon's farm and when his barn tipped over, all the maize come down the river. He lost a tractor in that flood too. The water was so strong it broke the wheels off it and we never found them.

'Mr Toby Nixon's property on the B road at Jarrahmond suffered severely. A gulch was created which engulfed his house and 50 acres of land valued at £70 an acre.' This was the highest flood in the history of Orbost. After having been battered with heavy logs and trees and taking the strain of the accumulated debris as the flood waters rose, the centre pier of the Snowy River bridge finally collapsed, causing a gap of 120 feet. The bridge had been open to traffic since 1922. Enormous losses were involved through the destruction of crops. Hay and maize were washed out to sea, roads and bridges were ruined along with machinery. However some of the live-stock escaped drowning. 'Percy Nixon found one of his big Queensland bullocks held high in the fork of a tree, whither it had been carried by the flood. It was rescued by men standing in water waist deep felling the tree, and the bullock was still alive.'[4]

One year after the floods we were working at Jimmy Nixon's at Orbost, putting in a trench through a cow-yard. We'd gone down about seven feet when we come across a big patch about three feet each way, all yellow with old bones and ashes, and I called out to Jimmy to come and have a look. We'd found an old Aboriginal oven. The silt had built up over the years and I dug right in under and got to where the fire finished, then down about another foot to the soil underneath. That's the only oven I've seen in Gippsland—the Snowy will pack up and wash out all of a sudden—not like up on the Murray, there's plenty of ovens to be seen up there.

In the 1951 floods at Orbost the water was brushing under the bridge and the cattle coming down in the river; well their horns were knockin' into the bridge, so we got forked sticks and as they come down we pushed their heads under so they could get out on to the higher ground over the other side of the bridge. One year two hundred cattle went out to sea at Marlo. I can remember another flood when a big pile of rubbish built up in one of the paddocks and a cow got up on top of that and stayed there till the water went down. Jimmy took hay out to that cow every day in his boat.

They've had trawlers to clear the trees away that have gone into the sea, swept from the Snowy. There's even been a house go out to sea. I've seen the Snowy rise six inches in half an hour—doesn't take long to come up.

Y'know Ethel can drive a tractor? Jimmy Nixon taught 'er, and when the paddocks were getting cleared Ethel hopped up there and drove while the tray was loaded with rubbish.

During the early 1930s Reggie Thorpe's wife died at Lake Tyers while she was having a baby and so did Edwin O'Rourke's wife, Sylvia. Edwin was Neddy and Eliza's son. Reggie and Edwin both had permission to be working at the station then, but the wages for them all had been cut down, because of the Depression I s'pose, and it wasn't a happy place there. Some of the families left when the Board said they could, but they had a hard time outside too.

During the Depression the men's salary was reduced and, when objections were raised, the Board issued no arguments against any worker wishing to leave his house on the station and return to his own country, forbidden to him for so long. Families regarded by the Board as not having enough Aboriginal blood—not dark enough—were expected to leave the station. In 1932 there were three families camping on the shore of the lake opposite the settlement, but complaints were sent to the Board by members of the white community. Several of the families who had been brought to Lake Tyers station from the Wimmera district returned to their old hometowns and camps. The number of people who left Lake Tyers certainly reduced the government maintenance costs, although sale of produce from the station contributed to covering expenses.

The families who returned to the Antwerp area in the Wimmera, lived in huts and mia-mias, poorly clad and fed. The officer in charge was moved to write of these 'unfortunate people', who some time ago had been transferred to Lake Tyers but had been allowed to return to Antwerp and were facing the winter of 1934, that 'these young children especially are in for a very bad time for the want of proper food and clothing.' There were 67 people living 'anywhere and everywhere in the Antwerp old Mission Station's grounds'.

In the same year, the manager at Lake Tyers station, Major Glen, was concerned about the deplorable delay by Pentridge in supplying the clothing 'for our natives'. The clothing was made by the prisoners for the Aborigines. Glen declared some of the station men were literally in rags and he was ashamed of them being seen by the outside community. Which of course, they were.

Unrest continued on Lake Tyers. Wages did not improve, the members of the Board were not in favour of 'the natives' growing their own vegetables, nor did they want fences around the cottages, unless they could be properly constructed and uniform. Tobacco supplies were cut and free dental treatment was stopped. Visiting times to the station by tourists were more strictly regulated.

The situation became a cause of rebellion and it was said a penal settlement could not be established without 'trebling' the staff. Members of the Protection Board faced the men of Lake Tyers in January of 1936, where they were assembled to hear the conditions under which they must live if they chose to continue residing on the station. If a man left to make a living outside, he must take his family. Once gone from the station, they could not return. Those remaining in their houses at the station must obey the rules and directions set down for the management of the settlement.

The men were told the Board was seriously considering forming a station where the work would be much harder and the conditions much less attractive; the same threat used eight years ago and referring to the same place of punishment, Tortoise Head Island.[5]

Lake Tyers Portraits

ROUND ABOUT CENTENARY TIME*, A WELL-KNOWN ARTIST WENT TO LAKE Tyers to do portraits of some of the Aborigines living there. They were done at Tooloo Arm where this artist was staying at a sort of guesthouse. It was a pub in the early days. At Tooloo, y'know, the fish come up there and spawn and when the young are ready they go down to Lake Tyers again. The tourists come there now to water-ski and have picnics, different to what it was when these blokes had their paintings done.

The artist was Australian Percy Leason and he painted the portraits of thirty-one Aborigines in 1934. The collection was known as, 'Victoria's Last Full-Blood Aboriginals'.[1]

Bob Andy took the people across the lake in his boat and they walked through the wattles and stringy-barks to the house when it was their turn to be painted. Bob was from New South Wales originally, from Walligah Lake. He was a very smart man, good at making boomerangs for sale at the station. A good footballer, he played in the ruck when I was centre and, when we played, we had a little bloke called Dainty Bond who was about three feet six and as light as a feather. He'd use his weight and just bounce off 'em and we used to laugh and say, 'Go on Dainty, get into 'em, don't let 'em do anything to a little blackfella like you.'

There was old Adam Cooper who had himself done by the artist. He worked for some of the white farmers even though he only had one good leg, the other was wooden. When he was a young fella he was jumping the hurdles and landed on a razor, and blood poisoning set in and he had his leg off at Bairnsdale Hospital. He was well liked, was Adam. His father was Dick, a real wild bloke and a hard one to tame, took years and years to tame 'im down. He'd pull out a boomerang and let them have it if there was any arguments. The young 'uns had to listen to the elders then and couldn't just go around and pick an argument. Dick was tall and wiry and he carried a bag made of possum or kangaroo skin with the good and bad spirit stones in it.

Hector Bull was the son of Billy the Bull. Hector had a brother Billy and a sister Clara. Now Hector played the gum-leaf, just like most of the Kurnai. He played the leaf outside Young and Jackson's pub in Melbourne for years, just stand there with his hat turned down for anyone to throw two bob in. Toby Nixon saw Hector there one time when he called into Young and Jackson's. He asked him how he was goin' and give him two bob, and Toby met some blokes he knew in the pub and started talking about the gum-leaf music and he told them, 'That fella outside can damn near make that leaf

* The Centenary of Victoria, 1934.

LAKE TYERS PORTRAITS

Adam Cooper (The La Trobe Collection, State Library of Victoria).

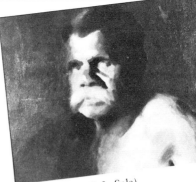

Hector Bull (J. L. Sala).

Clara Hunt (neé Bull) (The La Trobe Collection, State Library of Victoria).

Julian 'Dingo' Hood (J. L. Sala).

Harry Hayes (J. L. Sala).

Laurie Moffatt (J. L. Sala).

Edward Foster (The La Trobe Collection, State Library of Victoria).

Thomas Foster (The La Trobe Collection, State Library of Victoria).

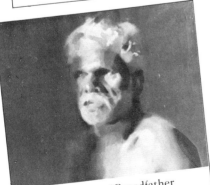

William Johnson (Grandfather Johnson) (The La Trobe Collection, State Library of Victoria).

Charley Green (The La Trobe Collection, State Library of Victoria).

talk.' Someone said, 'No one can play the leaf these days.' 'O.K.,' says Toby, 'if you want to make a bet I'll stake the wager and give it all to that fella out there.' So out they all went and Hector told them to pick what they wanted him to play. And he did, he played everything they asked for. The most popular song was 'Tipperary'.

THE HOOD FAMILY

There were four brothers in the Hood family and Dingo (Julian) was the eldest. Their mother could sing like a nightingale and she could play the organ for the singing at St John's on the mission. Some of the Hoods had their portraits done at Tooloo.

HARRY HAYES

Harry Hayes was the son of one of the first tribesmen that went to Lake Tyers. We were told what a great tracker the old fella was, goin' after the horse and sheep thieves. Him and a couple of other black trackers found sheep thieves had tied the legs of the sheep together and carried them out of a property so's there wouldn't be tracks for them to follow. Another time the police got the old fella to track a couple of white blokes. Well, he was in front of the police going ahead on his horse, when he was sure he seen the sun shinin' on the barrel of a gun way up in a tree. He didn't let on he saw this and kept goin' until he saw the bloke was in the tree. He just went right past, then gave the warning to the others coming up behind him. The prisoner told him after that he had his gun on him and if he had looked up he would have shot him.

LAURIE AND FOSTER MOFFATT

Laurie and Foster Moffatt were grandsons of old Charlie and Nora Foster. Laurie was always a great one for getting around, but he'd never go anywhere without his coat. I saw a photo of him during the Centenary, standing in Bourke Street watching the crowd go by. Another time in Melbourne I knocked into him and asked him what he was doing in the city and he said, 'You'll see me shaking hands with the Governor-General,' and I asked him, 'How will you get to do that?' Laurie just said, 'Don't you worry.' And do you know, that night his photo was in the *Herald* shaking hands with the Governor-General. How he got there I don't know. He was a good singer, a tenor—he had a beautiful set of teeth—he was in the St John's choir. At one of the Back to Lakes Entrance gatherings Sir Albert Lind was talking to the people when along come Laurie in a white shirt and bow tie, as large as life, and he waves to Sir Albert. 'How are you Laurie? I'll have a word with you later,' says Sir Albert. He was a Member of Parliament then. I was working in Sydney when the last Olympics was on and Ethel and me were shoppin' to buy a souvenir and the first thing Ethel spots is a plate with Laurie's photo on it.

Three Lake Tyers men visited Melbourne for the celebrations in December but they were sent back to the station by the Board Secretary and police.[2]

EDWARD FOSTER

Edward Foster was painted too; he was Laurie's uncle. Edward had the old tribal scars across him and those wounds gave the poor old fella some trouble. He would be about sixty years old when he was painted. A couple of his grown-up sons were painted too. 'Course, y'remember Edward's mother was Nora who come from Western Australia.

WILLIAM JOHNSON

William Johnson, well everyone always called him Grandfather Johnson, he must have been over seventy when he had his portrait done. Y'remember he was one of old Kitty and Larry's sons? He married Maggie McDougall, a sister of Johnny the Guide who married Bella O'Rourke. See the connection? Grandfather Johnson could talk the language. He would have been born while his mother was rearin' up Billy Thorpe and George Thomas.

(left to right) **William Johnson (Old Grandfather Johnson), Dick Northrope, Henry Thomas (Ethel Pepper's brother), _____ Burns** (Stratford Historical Society).

He was a great canoe-maker and could turn a boomerang better than any of 'em. There's a photo of him climbing on a tree to strip a canoe in the Folk Museum at Bairnsdale. As he got older, Grandfather Johnson would go off the station and go around the old camping places—often to places like Metung. The old people travelled all round that place when there were plenty of monkey bears and yams in the hills—all they wanted. Y'never see them now, that's all finished. They used the reeds in Chinamen's Creek to catch the ducks—by cleaning out a good-sized reed, making sure of a good hole, then the tribesman would stick it in his mouth and hop in the water and breathe through the reed. They'd stay under the water a long time like that and the ducks would come along and—bang—the Aborigines just grab the ducks' legs and pull 'im under.

On a bend past the hot water spring over-lookin' the creek there were once two big rocks—they called them the Red Rocks—well they just sat there on the point, must have been there for hundreds of years I suppose. The

Aborigines had a story about those rocks. Some of the tribesmen caught a lot of fish and they took them up on the top of this hill to cook them. 'Course they had their *merrigarn* with them—that's their dingo. They were their dogs in the early days and wherever the blackfellas camped the old *merrigarns* would keep nit for 'em and bark if there was anyone about who wasn't s'posed to be. The people knew that if ever those dingo dogs talked instead of barkin' they'd turn the blackfellas into stone. They believed that. Well this time the Aborigines had a lot of fish, so much they could hardly eat it all, but they didn't give any to the *merrigarns* or their pups, they just kept eating it and throwing the bones into the fire. The dogs hung around, nosing about looking for a feed of fish, but those blackfellas was greedy and wouldn't give them any. Two of the *merrigarn* spoke. 'Don't y'think we're hungry too? You throw all your bones in the fire and eat the fish, why can't you feed us?' As soon as those dogs spoke to them, the blackfellas all turned into stones and they rolled all the way down the hill and settled near the water. Those stones were there for years and only in the last fifteen years or so they went into the creek. One of the big stones was about fifteen feet high, round like a ball, and it had sort of heads stickin' out on it.

There was a family called Gilsenan, a white family, and their daughter is Cora Waters. Cora's grandfather was in that area when Billy Thorpe and George Thomas went out of Lake Tyers to earn their living amongst the whites. Over the years the Aborigines have been sent off the missions and sent back on again, then off again and back, and sometimes they were sick and hungry, or couldn't get work, didn't have enough money and their little kids were sick, or the Welfare would take them—all those things went on, and the Gilsenans always held out a helping hand to those people. When the tourists started to go round Bancroft Bay in the boats, Cora's father had afternoon teas for them, and often some of the Aborigines were there and they'd do their singing and boomerang throwing for the tourists. Now old Billy Johnson worked for the Gilsenans; he lived there too, must have been in the 1940s. He was a real nice old gentleman; always a proud sort of man. He always carried boomerangs round with him, ready to sell. When the people come to Gilsenans' place, Grandfather Johnson always had a supply made up, and he'd demonstrate how to throw the boomerang, and he'd teach the white people how to use it. He always walked round barefooted, in old clothes, because he reckoned the tourists didn't expect to see an old blackfella well dressed in a collar and tie and hat. That wasn't the natural way.

Well, one time he was back at Lake Tyers when he left there for his holiday to go to New South. He come over the lake in his canoe then walked along the morass, swan-eggin'. He come in to see our daughter Eileen and he said to her, 'Hey girl, will y'make a billy of tea for me?' He held out this little billy-can and Eileen took the lid off and there were all these swan eggs. She said, 'How can I do that, you've got the billy full of eggs.' Well, Grandfather Johnson had a good laugh; he was teasing her. He brought the eggs for Eileen. Anyway, she fixed a good feed for him and off he went. That was the last time any of us saw him, poor old fella.

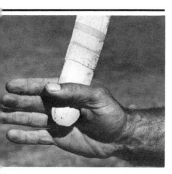
The first position of the hand for boomerang throw (Lin Onus).

My sister Alice was comin' home from her holidays and she met Grandfather Johnson at Narooma, and said she'd take him back to Lake Tyers with them, and they were to pick up a bus the next morning. They couldn't get beds for the night anywhere, so they camped out. They made a fire in the scrub back from the bridge. When Alice woke up in the morning, Grandfather Johnson was dead—his hand was a bit burnt by the camp fire. They got the

101

police and Alice had to explain to them why they were there and who they were. Old Billy Johnson was buried at Narooma.

McCormack made a song in Metung about the old fella and Slim Dusty has it on a record. In that song he says old Grandfather Johnson put the bite on 'im for money for tobacco if he ever met him in town. Then one time he had to tell the old fella he was broke himself. Old Grandfather Johnson looked at him and grinned, put his hand in his pocket and pulled out some notes and silver and put it in his hand and laughed at the look on his face. That song is a true story. Old Grandfather Johnson would give his last penny away.

ANGELINE McRAE

Angeline McRae was one of the women who were painted and she said when it was done she was young. Angeline said she'd like to see that portrait now.

CLARA BULL

Clara Bull was another of the women. She married a Carter and Alfred was her son, the bloke Captain Newman fixed with the gum-leaves treatment*. Clara later married a Hunt.

CENTENARY CELEBRATIONS

Now I mentioned about the Melbourne celebrations for the Centenary. Well we had a few things going in Gippsland too. The Duke of Gloucester come tourin' through, to meet the people and see the country, and everybody tried to get a look at him, but a lot missed out. Some of the Aborigines from Lake Tyers station were allowed out to see him.

During the Duke of Gloucester's tour of Gippsland in October 1934, he visited the show grounds at Orbost where 'a wonderful crowd assembled' to welcome him. The Duke was entertained at the grounds and later, 'whilst having afternoon tea the Duke was told of the Aboriginal Gum Leaf Band and he immediately expressed a desire to hear it. Efforts were hurriedly made to round up the musicians, but to the disappointment of the Duke it was found that they had left the ground earlier for the mission station.' Some hours later on the return trip to Melbourne, the Duke was able to meet a number of the residents from Lake Tyers. At the junction of the Lake Tyers road and the Prince's Highway 'the whole of the Aborigines from the mission station had been assembled in charge of Major Glenn and Mrs Glenn. As the Royal car approached, the Aborigines danced with joy to the accompaniment of vociferous yells. They swarmed around the Royal car and the Duke was immensely pleased with the welcome, and also the opportunity of seeing the few remaining full-blooded Aborigines of Victoria.'[3]

CHARLIE GREEN

Charlie Green was the father-in-law of my cousin Reggie Thorpe and he was a wonderful old fella. Everyone liked him. I suppose he was one of the mob from Tyers who saw the Duke. Old Charlie grew a shortish sort of beard sometimes, then he'd clean it off again. When his painting was done he had a beard. He was still a great runner and hurdler then.

* See page 84.

CHAPTER THIRTEEN

From Under the Rule at Lake Tyers

JUST BEFORE THE 1939–45 WAR, HUNDREDS OF TOURISTS WENT THROUGH the Lake Tyers station and the Aborigines entertained them in the hall with concerts, and the Gum-Leaf Band was still popular. The first one come from New South Wales. The Stewart brothers had it in 1917 and Baker Stewart married Ethel's sister Dolly. That band stayed around the district for years. A lot of Aborigines played the leaf at the concerts and Tommy Foster would put on an exhibition of fire-making, getting the fire going with his bark and stick, and the white people lit up their cigarettes from his fire.

When the war started, about thirty-seven men volunteered from Tyers and twenty-six passed the medical examination and they were right. They had a coupla weeks training in drill before they went off. They had a leaf band amongst themselves and they used to play at the AIF recruiting centres. There'd be a lotta white blokes in the army remember our boys playin' the leaf in camp.

During the war Reggie Thorpe's boy Vernon, at Tyers, won the John Batman Cup for the best essay written by any child from an Aboriginal school in Australia, and the Chief Secretary presented the cup to Vernon. Funny thing that, because in about the 1880s Eliza Thorpe's daughter Bella had her writing sent to England to show them how the Aborigines could write.

Braggin Scott and Grandfather Johnson's wife Maggie died during those years.

umbo (Lindsay) Pepper, aged fteen years.

Auntie Julia and Con Edwards went from the station with their children and Con worked at the Munitions, so did Jamsie Scott. Several families went to Orbost and worked on farms. That's where Bella, Eliza Thorpe and Neddy O'Rourke's daughter, died, up on Nixon's farm. They gave her a lovely funeral.

After the war our two sons Les and Jumbo played footy for Newmerella and one time, when we went to Lake Tyers station to play there, I had a bit of a go with Len Rule. I think he was the farm manager then. See, a lot of the fellas at Tyers were related to a lot of the Aborigines that didn't live on the station; years ago Ethel's brother Billy and my cousin Harry Booth said they didn't like to play against our people on the station when they played for Newmerella, but they couldn't stay on the mission so they had to play against 'em. Anyway there wasn't any hard feelings amongst us. But this day the team went to Lake Tyers to play, who pulls me car in but Len Rule. Well, there was a good crowd of locals at the station to see the match, sittin' round waiting for the start, see, some of the whites had bottles of drink and the Aborigines weren't allowed to drink then, if you was caught givin' drink— the publicans did sometimes—you was in trouble.

Well, Len Rule says to me, 'You haven't got no grog in your car to bribe our blokes with, have you?' I said to him, 'Mr Rule, don't talk to me like that. Look at the white men over there drinkin' it in front of the Lake Tyers men,' and I pointed to a bloke chuckin' a bottle, an empty one with a bit in it, 'and what's that bloke throwin' around over there? Why don't you talk to your white people first? You got the wrong man Mr Rule I don't carry that around and our team don't have it. I'm training 'em and grog is out. Now my brother-in-law is in there and my two boys, and I'm goin' in too and that's it.' And I did. I can't remember if we won or lost.

Len Rule and his wife were at Lake Tyers a few years before the war and didn't finish up until late in the fifties. He was farm manager and finished up manager. He was only a baker before he went on to the station so he knew nothing about farmin', and he told me out of his own mouth he used to give the men a handful of grass seed to put in a pocket, and when they walked around they was to just drop it around. If he was any sort of farm manager he could have done the right thing and sown that grass seed in the winter amongst the grass, but you got to sow it in quantities—harrow it into the ground, do the job properly. He didn't know that.

Len Rule owned a farm before he enlisted in the 1914–18 War and afterwards he returned to farming on a Soldier Settlement Block. He farmed at various places in Gippsland until, during the Depression, he learned baking in his father's shop. He was employed at the Lake Tyers station in 1935. He retired in 1958 but was re-employed by the Board for some years, to 'manage farming interests'. During his term at Lake Tyers, Rule acquired a farm five miles from the Aboriginal Station.

One time Dingo Hood was given a pass from the manager to do some bean pickin' at Orbost . . . now, y'see, on the station the men got a pay a long way under what we was getting outside, and it wasn't enough to get decent clothes for their families or extra food, so in the season they all tried to get permission to work on beans, maize and peas . . . so Dingo left his family on the station, but instead of going back when his pass was up, he stayed two more days and went back home with a fistful of money. Now that man had disobeyed the rules and because he was late . . . he'd 'ave got into trouble if he'd been two hours late if they'd caught him . . . Dingo was told to get off Lake Tyers. Rule hunted him off the station, he was hounded down like a dingo. Anyway he kept racin' round, keepin' behind them, they even fired off gunshots into the trees. What would have happened if he'd been up one of them trees? They got the police to get him off, and he wasn't allowed back for a long time, but he used to sneak in and go to his house to give the family money he earned outside.

When the Housing Commission first came about, there were supposed to be houses for Aborigines and some of the families were all pushed off Lake Tyers by Len Rule, there were six empty houses there, and those people had to make their own way. Well all they could do was camp, they had no money to buy houses or rent while they waited for jobs and for the Housing Commission places. Well, we had six inches of rain and these people went to the top of Bunga Hill where Mary Harrison (Bob Andy's daughter) lived with her family in their house. The only dry spot was Dickie Harrison's place and all these people were there, some in bark shelters. Mary Harrison went down to Cora Waters and brought her back to her place where those people were walking round like wet shags while those six houses sat empty at Lake Tyers.

Children with Cora Gilsenan-Waters at a Christmas picnic near Lake Tyers.

Cora and Mary saw Len Rule but he wouldn't let them come back, so they said they'd put it in every paper in Australia and that would give the show away. Well, Mr Felton from the Board in Melbourne come up, and he got blankets and food from the station and took it up to Bunga Hill for the people. There were kids carted off to hospital and women went off with pneumonia and Rule never had the decency to get the big bus and take them to Lake Tyers. The men built bark mia-mias until they got houses. Now that's the sort of man Len Rule was.

There was a white bloke called Millikin on the station in charge while Rule was there, and from what I heard no one liked the way he treated the Aborigines—he didn't stay long. Well time and time again Cora Gilsenan-Waters helped the Aborigines; one Christmas she got all the children out near old Grandpa Thorpe's favourite camp site and gave them a great Christmas party. Stewart Murray* and meself got talking and we decided it was time we did something for that woman, and Stewart said we ought to get a decoration for her and I said that was a good idea. Stewart went all round the *koories* in Melbourne and I did Gippsland and we got about four or five pages of names and Bruce Evans, M.P., and Peter Nixon helped us. Cora was awarded the M.B.E.

THE LAKE TYERS PLANNING AND ACTION COMMITTEE

The Lake Tyers Planning and Action Committee had some meetings to try and improve living conditions and work somethin' out for the young people coming on. Ethel and me were invited to go and, at one of the meetings in 1966, Charlie Carter told the meeting a hospital was needed, a small one on the station, to care for the sick and the old. They had to use a tractor to get Mrs Rule from her place when anyone was sick. Someone said transport was a terrible problem for the residents; Choppy Hayes thought Tyers could be a good trainin' place for the young fellas to learn farming, the older men living off the station would go back to train them; a telephone was needed . . . there were a lot of things. Fishing, a timber mill, peas and beans—all these things were talked about. Dickie Harrison said the road to Lake Tyers could be made three to four miles shorter and that job would give employment. Well that short-cut road was a tricky one, because the residents wanted that; it

* Stewart Murray at that time was a member of the Aboriginal Advancement League, Melbourne.

105

would save a good long walk for them. Len Rule was another one of the people invited to the meeting, and when I said the road could go through Burnt Bridge he said, 'You wouldn't be able to get up that way . . . that's a steep hill and when it rains it's greasy.' I said gravel could be used on it and then they'd have their short cut . . . he was heading for the good road to come out through his place near the station. If the road went through Snuff Gully to Lake Tyers it was a short cut of sixteen miles. The residents wanted it. They didn't get it. Len Rule got what he wanted and they call it Rule's Road now and the Aborigines on Lake Tyers never got their short cut.

A few years before those meetings some of the families out of the station were real hungry and the people on the station tried to get food out to them, but they got caught at it . . . our people would feed our own, not let them starve.

Well, someone said one time the peas and beans grown on the land at Tyers had topped the Melbourne market, and I said I'd help with them. Tyers is frost-free and passionfruit would grow there too. Well, we sent a letter to the Aborigines Welfare Board and told them Sunkist Frozen Food Company would provide seed for a trial planting and arrange the marketing of the crop. The Bairnsdale and District Aboriginal Affairs Committee was with me, and the idea was to rent ten acres on Lake Tyers. Well it didn't get off the ground. I knew in me own heart and soul it said in one of the government gazettes there was better places to grow beans than at Lake Tyers . . . This crop I was talkin' about was straight after the Caulfield Cup time, three months ahead of the other crops. If they'd let me go, we could have Lake Tyers different to what it is today.

THE LAKE TYERS ABORIGINAL TRUST

Then they brought in the Ministry of Aboriginal Affairs for Victoria instead of havin' the Aborigines Welfare Board* and after a while the government handed over the title deeds to Lake Tyers Reserve to the people living there. They were members of the Tyers Trust, see? Well, then those

* This had replaced the Central Board for the Protection of Aborigines in 1958. Alan West worked under the Welfare Board at Lake Tyers for about six months until he and other members of the Board resigned; Alick Jackomos, who was Liaison Officer for the Aboriginal Advancement League, transferred to Lake Tyers as the Officer in Charge, appointed to the staff of the Welfare Board until this body was replaced by the Ministry of Aboriginal Affairs six months later.

Lake Tyers Station, 1974.

people didn't have to ask for permission for their relations and friends to visit them and there were some new houses put up with a bathroom in them instead of the people having to go to the bath-house that was there. Some of the people had a long distance to walk to that bath-house.

The residents on the 4000 acres of ground at Tyers had to make a go of farmin' the place—now y'cannot put a city bloke on land and say, 'Go to it boy, this is yours,' because that man can't run that farm. He's gotta be taught. A committee was elected to manage the place, and Charlie Carter was the first chairman, with a white man manager of the farm and the men working under him. The year Father Butscher went there with me the beans were beautiful, crisp and juicy, and extra men were working on them for a fast pick, then they were snap-frozen. One of the pickers had come down to Tyers for the bean season from Hookers Creek.

Father Butscher had been with our people in Western Australia and he was interested to see how the farm was going at Tyers, see the machinery and the stock and meet some of our people. When we went on to the station through the big timber archway the old kookaburras were laughing away in the trees. One of the tractors come along with some of the fellas waving at us, they had a load of wood, and we met another lot working and I introduced Father Butscher to these blokes. Old Con Edwards was in the town at his house, so I knocked him up and he come and talked to us. When we passed the house where the white manager lived, Con said, real proud, 'He's the manager, but I'm over him.' We had a look in St John's and Con showed the pews, the ones made by the old people when John Bulmer was there. On the wall they had a copy of the title deeds of Lake Tyers, hanging in a frame. There's an honour board in there, too, for World War I, and the five names on it are Aborigines. My Dad's name is on that board.

We met Charlie Carter outside and had a bit of a talk . . . a week later he was dead . . . and Con wasn't boss for very long after—he died the same year.

Rev. Father Joseph Butscher and Phillip Pepper.

'It was not yet possible to measure the success of Lake Tyers Aboriginal settlement as at present administered nor could its success be measured in terms of financial expenditure;

'This is how Rev. Fr Butscher saw the settlement when on a recent visit to glean first-hand information on a project for which he has an inbuilt appreciation and understanding.

'Fr Butscher is a member of the Pallottine Order and worked with Catholic Missions in the Kimberleys for 13 years . . .

'At Lake Tyers Station he spoke with the manager (Mr C. Gaskin) and Mr Con Edwards, chairman of the Committee of Management . . .

'He saw bean growing, cattle raising, and sheep farming in operation, but felt that fishing had possibilities as a source of employment and income for aborigines around Lake Tyers.

'In trying to understand their ways Fr Butscher acknowledges an acceptance of aborigines' instincts to share their possessions and for this reason sees more hope of integrating them into society through their own communities, rather than by assimilation . . .

'He said it was important that enterprises where aborigines can undertake work comparably with Europeans be encouraged and completed.

107

'Unless this were done, their dignity and pride as human beings is lost, he said.'[1]

In 1968 the Ministry for Aboriginal Affairs replaced the Aborigines Welfare Board and the newly-appointed Director was instructed to disregard previous policies. He was to look for the answers to the acknowledged social and economic disadvantages besetting Victorian Aborigines.

The Aboriginal Lands Act 1970 was designed to provide a basis on which Aboriginal people 'may regain a rightful place in our multi-racial society'.

Lake Tyers did not become the property of all Victorian Aborigines but 'it does, however, symbolise a principle of the ownership of Aboriginal Reserves by those Aborigines who live on the Reserves'. The other Reserve was Framlingham in the western district of Victoria.

The provisions of the Act are that all residents of the Lake Tyers Reserve who had lived there since 1 January 1968, or who had been admitted on the authority of the Aboriginal Council at Lake Tyers, became eligible for inclusion on the register of the Lake Tyers Aboriginal Trust.

Adult Trust members were entitled to 1000 shares, and every person under twenty-one years, 500 shares. A valuation of the property in 1970 showed each share to be valued at approximately $6.37. These shares became the personal property of the holders. Conditions within the Act prevent non-Aboriginal people from easily obtaining any shares if a holder wishes to sell or transfer. Before any land at all can be sold, a special notice must be given at a general meeting of the Trust, followed by a unanimous vote at the meeting which discusses the special resolution. The Act states clearly that the dissent of only one person will prevent the sale of land.

In July of 1971 the Victorian Governor presented to the Lake Tyers Aboriginal Trust, the unconditional title deeds to the 4000 acres of land, originally the Lake Tyers Mission Station and of latter years known as the Aboriginal Reserve.[2]

Lake Tyers
24th July 1971

Souvenir Cover, 'Presentation of Land Title To Aboriginal Trust', 24 July 1971, Lake Tyers.

The Australian Aboriginal Vote

IN THE EARLY DAYS WHEN REV. HAGENAUER AND REV. BULMER WERE IN charge of the missions in Gippsland, they got some of the men who were eligible to put their names down so they could have a vote. One of those blokes who put 'is name down was Billy Thorpe and I can remember being with him when he went to vote. That was before the First World War. My Dad Percy Pepper was voting too.

SENATOR BILL BROWN

Now that fact caused a big row at a meeting I was at in Bairnsdale when Senator Bill Brown was there representing the Minister for Aboriginal Affairs.

In June 1974, Senator Bill Brown visited Cann River, Orbost, Nowa Nowa, Bairnsdale and Lake Tyers and on behalf of the Minister of Aboriginal Affairs he examined the conditions under which the Aborigines were living, in regard to such things as education, availability of work, housing and health. It was established the conditions for the Aborigines were generally deplorable in terms of housing, health services, education and employment opportunities. The meeting with the Aborigines in Bairnsdale was chaired by Nessie Skuta, Gippsland representative for the National Aboriginal Council, and was attended by the residents of the area, Aborigines and white people.[1]

At that meeting Bill Brown made out that it was his government, the Labor Party, had made it possible for the Aborigines to vote. I pointed out to him that wasn't true, that my grandfather was voting before the war and he argued with me, using some bad language too—he said that wasn't right and I got pretty hot meself. Well he was so sure of himself he said he'd bet me one hundred dollars to a thousand those people didn't have the vote. He told me to put me money where me mouth was—who walks around with a hundred dollars in his pocket? Bill Brown said he would give the money to a charity I named if he lost the bet. If he's got that much dough to sling around why don't he give it, anyway? Well, I was pretty disgusted and upset and I walked out of that meeting. I said, 'One out all out. All us Koories stick together,' and when I went out they all come with me. I looked back and there was Nessie left sitting at the table by herself with Senator Bill Brown. There wasn't any Koories left to finish the meeting.

Some people say because I didn't say, 'Yes, I'll take that bet,' and shake a hand on it, that didn't make it a bet any more. To me that don't matter. He proved he didn't know about the Aborigines voting by wanting to bet on it.

I rang me old mate Peter Nixon the Member of Parliament and told 'im what happened and asked him to get the proof, and he did.

From the inception of responsible government in 1855 the same electoral laws applied to Aborigines and non-Aborigines.[2]

Peter Nixon contacted Bill Brown and told him that I named the Save the Childrens' Fund at Nowa Nowa to get the thousand dollars. He wouldn't pay up.

There were two articles in the Melbourne papers about the bet and there was a couple in the local papers. It was discussed in Parliament and took up pages in their Hansard and it's all there for anybody to read what Senator Brown said. Everybody knows what he said at that meeting, we all know, and he hasn't paid up his money to this day. Those little kids could have done with a thousand dollars.

You know how he got out of it? He said when he spoke at the meeting about the Aborigines voting he was talking about adult franchise for national elections. 'Far as we was concerned the argument was about the Aborigines voting round about 1910 or 1912, somewhere there. My Grandfather's voting had nothing to do with the Labor Party then.

As far as we were concerned that was another promise broken by a politician and there's been plenty of those.

On 9 July 1974, David Brunton in his column, 'In black and white', Melbourne Herald, *brought to the notice of readers, the situation as it happened:*

> *'Looks like Labor Senator, Bill Brown, has got more problems.*
>
> *'When he was in Gippsland last week representing Aboriginal Affairs Minister, Senator Cavanagh, he told a public meeting at Bairnsdale that if it hadn't been for pressure by a Labor Government, aboriginals might still not have the vote.*
>
> *'Local aboriginal leader, Phil Pepper, disputed this, and said he could remember his father voting as far back as 1908.*
>
> *'Senator Brown then challenged him to prove it with a bet of $1000 to $100 to go to any charity he cared to name.*
>
> *'Seems that Country Party MHR for Gippsland, Peter Nixon, has been doing some checking for Mr. Pepper and has found that in Victoria aboriginals got the vote in 1855.*
>
> *'Get out the cheque book, Bill.'[3]*

The Bairnsdale Advertiser *on 18 July 1974 referred to the wager as a flippant offer which could cost Senator Bill Brown $1000. Mr Nixon told the* Advertiser *by telephone, that he had spoken with Senator Brown, who confirmed that he proposed to honour the 'debt'.[4]*

As the $1000 did not appear, Mr B. Snedden, M.H.R., was contacted and he approached Senator Brown during April 1975.

Senator Brown told Mr Snedden that his colleague raised the matter in the House of Representatives on 30 July 1974, to which he replied the following night. This can be found in the Senate Hansard of 31 July 1974, pages 678–82.

When forwarding this information to an enquirer, Senator Brown advised he had nothing to add.

In the Senate on 31 July 1974, Senator Brown stated there was only one newspaper report in the region and this had been checked by the

Parliamentary Library. The report appeared on the front page of the Bairnsdale Advertiser *on 27 June 1974. Senator Brown said it certainly contained no reference to any comment by him about where or when Aborigines did not receive a vote in Victoria.*[5]

The Victorian Year Book *of 1973 covers the voting rights of Victorians. Under the Victorian Constitution of 1855 Aborigines were not excluded from voting in Council and Assembly elections. Some restrictions would have prevented voters, both Aboriginal and white people, from voting in State elections as one of the conditions was that electors were required to be owners, lessees or occupying tenants of property of certain value. This was abolished in 1856, one reason being the presence of thousands of gold diggers not eligible to vote.*

As We Are

THE FEDERAL GOVERNMENT

DURING THE LAST FEW YEARS THERE'S BEEN CHANGES FOR THE ABORIGINES in Victoria and one was when the Ministry finished up and the Affairs come under the Federal government. When Reg Worthy was the Director during the Ministry time, they had an Advisory Council made up of Aborigines from different areas of Victoria and there was the opportunity to talk and be listened to, sometimes it did not do any good—talk—other times it did. They had a Lands Council too, but that got folded up quick smart.

The Ministry ceased to function as a State government instrumentality responsible for Aboriginal Affairs in Victoria on 11 January 1975: policy, planning and co-ordination was transferred to, and administered by, the Federal Department of Aboriginal Affairs, Victorian Regional Office, with area offices in Bairnsdale, Swan Hill, Shepparton and Morwell.[1]

WASTED MONEY

The housing business for Aborigines is one place where there has been, and still is, a lot of wasted money; y'see, real old houses are bought, then they spend thousands of dollars doing them up and by the time they pay for it all they could have had a new house cheaper. A good bath was taken out of one house to be replaced, good light fittings went, a fireplace got modern heating and that wasn't necessary. When you run out of wood the people can get more, but instead they get a big bill all at once for the heater. A house needs reblocking, so it's throwing money away to repair walls or lift doors and those sort of things. I've known where a white bloke just lives around with an Aboriginal sheila and gets a house—now that is not right. Drains put in where they caused water to settle under a house, workmen entering a house while the occupiers were out and using their electricity, that's not right either. These wasted repair jobs are done by white blokes who are getting paid with the money allocated by the government for Aboriginal Affairs and it's money used up that could often be put to better use. Of course houses are needed, but sensible buying is necessary. If you haven't got a car, you don't need a garage built, do you? The Ministry for Housing knows there are disturbing facts about the situation in East Gippsland and it continues. We've written letters and we've talked to Members of Parliament about the waste.

Money is wasted on a lot of things . . . at one time there the Department of Aboriginal Affairs had an office in Box Hill costing something like $1000 a week to run and it wasn't used for twelve months. That money would have been better used for the people, like expert training in farming, training that should have been done at Lake Tyers . . . when they gave over Tyers they built a brick wall between them and the outside. Some of those white fellas didn't have enough brains to give themselves a headache, they wouldn't listen to the people.

Under the Aboriginal Affairs Act, which became effective in January 1968, there was a Minister, Director, and an Aboriginal Affairs Advisory Council, 'at least three members of which are aboriginals . . .' First meeting of the Advisory Council *(left to right)* C. Gilsenan-Waters, P. Pepper, R. Southby, M. Tucker, S. Davey, M. R. Worthy (Director), the Hon. E. Meagher (Minister), Rev. G. Pearson, L. Cooper, A. Booth, T. Emerson, H. Walsh, J. Gaskin.

GOOD AND BAD ABORIGINES . . . AND WHITES

Lionel Rose.

I could take you to over in New South Wales where Aborigines got beautiful homes—brick—and beautiful inside and they keep them like that, with a real flash car outside, brand spankin' new. This is what our people can do. They're not all dumb as some people think they are. 'Course we've got our share of poor people, under-educated Aborigines and the no-hopers too. Now this money that is paid to the unemployed for not working is no good, they should be given work like in the Depression when you got money from the government but you had to work for it; now they don't. They could pick the people up in buses and set them to work and they could beautify Australia. Some of these blokes, white and dark who work a double pension need a crack on the head with a *nulla-nulla*.

A dark man is more noticed drunk on the street than a white man drunk and they give the Aborigines a bad name. In the same way, some white men give the white community a bad name as far as the Aborigines see it. We have 'gin-men' come round for a young girl, hanging about lookin' for a dark girl. They're still about. White men give a bad impression in lots of ways, like one time when a few of us was workin' on beans and there was a white bloke there too and he made a humpy to live in. He got empty bean sacks and filled them with dry grass to use as pillows and mattress, and he lived like that. Well he'd go off and get drink for the men, all they wanted, with their wages, and he'd never give them any change either; he was on a good thing, eh? Some of us knew what he was up to. See, these fellas give the whites a bad name with us and they've been amongst us for a long time, these types. It gets that way sometimes, the Aborigines think all whites are the same.

At a meeting recently a white bloke, well-known in the Bairnsdale district, started on me about Lionel Rose, slinging off at him. He says, 'And where's all his money gone?' and I said, 'Y'don't need to worry about him, mate, he's got some invested. Lucky too, because a lot of these white blokes hangin' round him helped to use up his money.' So then he started on Sir Douglas

113

Nicholls. I said, 'Well he has got two medals, what you got, . . . a black gin.' See? That's the way some of 'em are.

As far as Victorian Aborigines are concerned the Aboriginal culture as it was is gone, but there is no harm in them knowing about it. We couldn't go back to it now, but it was religion and the Maker there, in that culture. The men who followed Nathaniel Pepper help our people now and they have evangelical services, preaching and singing. They are good Christian people and they go where they are needed and wanted, and being Christian doesn't stop you being proud of the culture the old people had. The young ones always listened to the elders then, but today they stand up and argue the point, think they know more. If we only had the elders of the tribes today as a force to educate our people. Now when they get into trouble they got these lawyers to get them out of it—and if we had the elders like they've got in Queensland and up north and west, they'd give 'em the waddy; it might make a lot more sense with our young. Y'get these radical blokes talking and not making much sense sometimes, and that's when the old people should be listened to.

My sister Sarah married Bennie Cruse (his father was a Red Indian, an Apache) and Ossie is their son. He is a Minister. When Ossie went outback to the Aborigines, his crowd couldn't show a photo or sing or pray or preach, not till the elder came, and when that man showed up with a rag around his head he put his hand up and everybody would go to their positions and the service could start. Ossie says in those outback places in the centre of Australia they had three separate choirs and they dressed in different colours for the different tribes and all barefooted. I said to Ossie, 'There's a lotta shoes needed for them,' and he said, 'No Uncle, they wouldn't want shoes there in the sandy desert, they wouldn't know how to wear them and they wouldn't want them either.' Ossie told us, 'You've never heard the singing so wonderful, they preach in their language and they can talk good English. They've got money and they're well dressed. There's more Christian Aboriginal people out among the wild people than what there are walking around here in Victoria and New South Wales. That's where you find the Christian mob, it's out there.'

There are other Aboriginal pastors belonging to the Evangelical Fellowship, and Lindsay Grant and David Kirk are a couple who have held meetings. Ethel and I have been over to Port August and they have big meetings there. People come from everywhere, out of the bush, further up the country, and from Queensland, New South Wales, and I met some from Roper River once, some from Darwin and the West. Couple of years ago I met a young fella from West Australia who had come out of the bush, and his mother and sisters were still living the tribal way. We talked about that and he didn't know whether it was better for them—to go out of their bush and live away from there, or to stay where they are. Where would his family be happiest most? How can you tell? It's like a jigsaw puzzle with one part missing.

Some of the yarns told there at the Fellowship meetings would make you cry. At one meeting at Port Augusta there was a woman there who was drunk and she had her two little boys with her, one each side. They led her in. When the people sang that final hymn, 'Come to Jesus Now', you could see the tears rolling down out of one of those kid's eyes while he was walking with his mother down to David Kirk.

The old fella, the father, he started to abuse David, and he said to him, 'What you doin' taking my old woman away. You shouldn't take her away, let

114

Rev. D. Nicholls (Sir Douglas) in foreground with Stewart Murray talking to David Anderson *(back to camera)* on their trip to Swan Hill.

her stop here, I want her for myself,' then he would take a couple of steps forward and sorta something seemed to hold him back and he'd bend down, making hard work of walking forward, then he turned around and looked back. I stood up and looked around and I could see all these drunken blokes at the back. This old fella kept shaking his head. Anyway, all the people kept singing this song, 'Come to Jesus Now', and he just stood there and cried like a baby. It must've been hitting him. After a while he abused the people.

Well, a coupla days later they had another meeting and David was singing and praying and this same old fella came in and walked straight up to David, knelt down there and apologised. I asked some other blokes about him after, and they said, 'He was the devil himself. If he can do it, we can do it too.' It just goes to show. You wouldn't believe it unless you saw it yourself.

We wanted to have these Fellowship meetings at Lake Tyers when Reg Worthy* was in Victoria, and they said if the people wanted that the government would support it. We wanted it, and it was allowed, and we had a big meeting. Everyone helped to make it a success. The Aborigines who worked on the land took vegetables to provide food and anything else they had, tents and blankets.

At one of the meetings Stewart Murray was saying some Aborigines were needing help, and he said some white people in the same area were in trouble and he didn't mind helping them. Our white people needed help same as our dark people and we did what we could for that family same as for the Aborigines.

When the Lands Council was on the go, we went to Swan Hill to see how a young bloke was getting on with his farm, to give any help and advice he wanted. It's good to lend a hand to a man who is trying to get along under his own steam, you help to fire him and you can stand back and say, 'Ah well,

* At that time Director of Aboriginal Affairs in Victoria.

look at the blokes I've helped to push off!' It's a good feeling. Trouble is, then you get dirt thrown back in your face because it gets said to you, 'What about all those living on the river-bank? What you doing about them?' What can you say about that? I say you've got to put all these fellas to work, just as they are working on the mills. Some of them we have got to get dried out. We need places for that. There are several houses on the go and doing well in this work. The thing is—if you can't help yourself, nobody else can help you.

You remember me talking about old Archie Pepper who lived at Ebenezer, too? Well, when he left the mission and went to Lake Boga to live, my Dad was there for a while. Now Archie's grandson Frank Stewart, he lives at Swan Hill and he has worked for our people, and he finished up being the Officer in Charge of the Aboriginal Affairs at Swan Hill. He was awarded the Order of Australia a few weeks after his mother died. She was Nellie Stewart and was going on for ninety-one years. I'm glad I saw her recently. We had a great old yarn about old times and the early days and y'know that old lady remembered a lot of things.

Granny Stewart's mother Jessie married Archie Pepper at Ebenezer and she told us she was born at the mission. She said,

> 'The church is still there. Mrs Jacobi used to come down and play the organ. Whether she's dead or not I don't know. We were always there, ready to sing . . . they were wonderful days at Ebenezer . . . my mother was very careful and so was my Daddy. If Daddy couldn't take us to church, if he had influenza or something, he'd be sitting outside wrapped up in a blanket in a chair in the sun, waiting for us to come home from church. Poor old Daddy at Ebenezer. "Are they coming yet, Arch?" my mother would say. "No, not yet." We would stay outside and wait until he saw us running home. He would never stay down there at the church, we knew Daddy was sitting waiting for us. Then he would ask us the text and where it was found in the Bible. We had to tell him all that. I've got Daddy's Bible yet.'

Granny Stewart told me about Rev. Kramer on the mission. She said, 'He was a German minister. I can just remember him and that's all. You see I was just a little girl at the time when he was at Ebenezer, but I can remember him. When Mr Kramer died, they called all the blackfellows up to stand and sing when he was going off, and they sang him out of this world, into the next. He died while they were singing a hymn to him. I was only a little girl, but I can still remember it . . . Mr Spieseke was a school teacher, he was Daddy's teacher, too. Mr Bogisch taught us at school. We left Ebenezer when I was about twelve, I think, and came to Boga.'

We talked about our different languages and Granny said *marmook* was father, and I told her we say *moongan*; we say *yuccan* for mother and Granny said they called their mother *barbook*, and she said sometimes they called blackfellows *goorie*. She said to me, 'I wish Daddy was alive. He could tell you all these things . . . there was a place called Pepper's Plains in the Wimmera, you know.' We don't know how the Plains got the name, it's still named that.

There is a photo of Nellie Pepper (Granny Stewart) in a book about the missions and she is very young in it, and I asked her how they got that picture, but she didn't know, only that someone had it at Dimboola. At Lake Boga where the family lived and had their own house—that paddock is still called Pepper's Paddock. There was a mission there at Lake Boga, started by

Granny Stewart and Phillip.

the Moravians before they had Ebenezer, and that's where Nellie's husband's father was before he went to Ebenezer, and when they had to leave that place most of the people went back to Lake Boga and Mystic Lake. When Nellie married Jackson Stewart, they lived at Boga too.

Some of the people at Ebenezer that Granny Stewart remembered were Pelham Cameron and his wife Blanche. (Pelham was brother to Donald Cameron who went to Ramahyuck.) There was Albert Coombes and his wife and Dick Kennedy and his wife, and Granny Stewart said the government gave them a farm each and Pelham lived on his till he died. She said, 'Oh, he worked hard, he sold all his wheat he used to grow. Dick Kennedy shifted down to the Murray later on and he was a good farmer.'

The Moravian Church or, more properly, the Church of the United Brethren, had been contacted in 1848 because of the disturbing reports of the disastrous effect colonisation was having on the Aborigines. In 1850 Rev. Taeger and F. Spieseke, a lay missionary at the time, were granted 363 acres of land at Lake Boga for a reserve. Unfriendly settlers and the discovery of gold and insufficient government support closed the mission six years later. Many of the Aborigines moved to Ebenezer when the mission was established. By that time Spieseke had been ordained so it was as the Rev. Spieseke that he began work at Ebenezer with Rev. Hagenauer.

Nellie Stewart was born at Ebenezer in 1887. The farming families she spoke of did not own the land. In 1891 a portion of the Ebenezer reserve was of no use to the station as it was entirely covered with mallee scrub, and several men applied for the use of this land and were granted occupation. These men worked their small farms and, when times were bad, they were employed by neighbouring farmers, still maintaining their own land. Coombes, Kennedy and Cameron lived there by permission of the Board for Protection of Aborigines and the land, house, horses and stock plus farming implements were the property of the Board, and they could not borrow money or raise loans on that which was not theirs. In 1895 Coombes was supplied with seed wheat and horse feed and the resulting crop belonged to the Board with the understanding that he would obtain for his labour a fair and reasonable share after harvest.[2]

The Aborigines, the missionaries and the station struggled on. Sickness, deaths and the new Acts of Parliament, which sent Aborigines with any white blood away from Ebenezer, reduced the population on the mission.

In 1904 the once fully-occupied and useful station of Ebenezer finally closed. The reserved land was handed back to the Lands Department. Bishop B. La Trobe, a Director of the Moravian Mission Board in Germany, said his Board would be grateful if the government would make a permanent reservation of the burial ground on the mission 'as five of our missionaries are buried there among some 150 of the blacks to whose temporal and spiritual welfare they have ministered'.[3]

Ramahyuck

THE HUNDREDTH ANNIVERSARY
OF NATHANIEL'S BURIAL

MARCH 1977—THAT WAS WHEN IT WAS ONE HUNDRED YEARS AGO THAT Nathaniel Pepper was buried at Ramahyuck. I wanted to have a memorial service for him but it was not easy to get into that ground because the reserved land for the mission was sold up years ago. We knew there were the graves of our people in there, behind the fences somewhere, and there were graves of some whites too.

There are eighty Aborigines and sixteen white people buried at Ramahyuck in the cemetery.* This is not at present (1979) a registered cemetery but the area and the access routes to the cemetery are on Crown Land. The last of the mission reserve was sub-divided in 1955 and the burial site merged into the general pattern of farmland.[1]

WHITE AND BLACK AT
RAMAHYUCK MISSION

Those whites were settlers who took up land near Ramahyuck and they went to the mission church. Their children went to the school with the Aborigines. The Dad told me he remembered playing around the place with the white kids and he was always nickin' off to some German people's farm to ride their old horse. He went there so much they nicknamed him Baumy. Elisabeth and Christian Baum's tombstone is one of the white graves at Ramahyuck. They had their house near Bony Point, just about at the meeting place of the Perry and Avon. That spot was a camp-site of the early Aborigines and is called Bony Point because of all the bones of Aborigines found there before Rev. Hagenauer started the mission nearby. When the Baums went to live there, the men from Ramahyuck and Rev. Hagenauer helped them to build their house. One of their sons married a daughter of Rev. Hahn who was a teacher at Ramahyuck.

Mrs Ken Baum said that her elderly relatives had described how the Aboriginal ladies would be all dressed in white for special occasions. They'd sail down the Avon to other church services, singing in beautiful harmony and the Baums would stand on the bank of the river to listen to them. The Baum family attended the mission church about four miles away from their home, and the children were pupils at the school along with the Aborigines and the Hagenauer children and other white children. Mr Hahn was the teacher then.[2]

---

* The deaths of the Ramahyuck Aborigines were reported by Rev. F. Hagenauer to the Board. The following names were repeated time and time again as each member of a family died. Few descendants of the residents are now living.

Cameron, Chase, Darby, Edwards, Fitchett, Foster, Gilbert, Hood, Hamilton, Jones, King, Login, Murray, O'Rourke, Pepper, Moffatt, Raymond, Rivers, Stephen, Scott, Kramer, Wood.

The names of eight of the white people were supplied by Councillor Laurie Hamlyn; these white people were buried between 1890–6.

Mr and Mrs Baum, Mrs Scholz, Mr and Mrs Bruse, Mr Hartwick and his two sons.

Phillip standing by a canoe tree on the old Ramahyuck property.

Young women of Ramahyuck Mission, 1870.

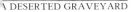

Nathaniel's gravestone, 1976.

George Hoffman, a good white bloke who got some of the Ramahyuck ground when it was split up—well I know him and he went around the place with me. His ground is on the river and he showed me trees where the natives had stripped canoes. One big tree had a fourteen-foot canoe taken off it—well over a hundred years ago by the way it's barking over—and others had barked over so far they must have had the canoes cut out three or four hundred years ago. Another tree had the bark cut out in a circle for a plate—they'd just chuck the ducks into the ashes and on to that plate for a feed. We didn't have permission that day to see the grave site. You have to do these things legal and you can't just go walkin' across a man's farm, so we got permission for me to have a look.

I got a bloke from Aboriginal Affairs in Melbourne to come down and go with me to see the cemetery. In the old days it had a fence around it but nothing is there. We could see where the white people was buried because a couple had old iron fences still there and broken headstones. Y'couldn't see where the Aborigines were buried though, except you could tell by the uneven ground. I had to find Nathaniel's stone, and I had a picture of Con Edwards standing beside Nathaniel's grave, taken when Con was a very young bloke. The trees were only saplings in that picture so I looked for those saplings only grown into trees, and when I found them I knew Nathaniel's stone had to be there somewhere. The ground was sunk where other Aborigines are buried but their wood crosses had rotted away a long time ago. Well, I found Nathaniel's stone with the grass and ground growing over it and we dug it out. I took some photos of it and some others round the cemetery. It wasn't any good leaving the stone propped up with something because the farmer's cattle could be roaming all over this place anyway, so we laid it down in the sunken part—Nathaniel's grave.

Ramahyuck Cemetery: Con Edwards standing by Nathaniel's gravestone, 1906.

I reckoned the cemetery should be preserved and I asked the Member of Parliament, Bruce Evans, to give a hand about it. We got in touch with the National Trust of Australia, but they couldn't classify individual graves and, as the grave mounds were what they called levelled and the site couldn't be seen, that was that—we couldn't get the cemetery made a historical place. The papers said Ramahyuck's remains, with the cemetery included, had been erased from the face of the earth. To us it isn't. Our people are there, many of them my relations. The proof they were there is in the canoe trees. You can't beat those; they're not invisible, you can touch them. And there's Nathaniel's gravestone. Part of the fence the old tribesmen built around the church is still there too. That place is part of the history of the Gippsland Aborigines and should be preserved.

Now I had to arrange a service for Nathaniel's anniversary and I reckoned a lot of Aborigines would come and whites too, especially any descendants of any buried there. Our Christian men got talking together and they knew how they would have the service . . . Ossie Cruse and the evangelical pastors would make the arrangements. The trouble was it was all right for me to go there or just one or two people, but when it come to having a lot of people for a service, that was different and the farmer wasn't happy about the idea—he didn't want that. I went to the Shire and told them the story and they said they could try and help. There was a Crown Land access track to the cemetery but it went over a creek, and if it was bad weather and the creek was flooded we couldn't get in, and anyhow you couldn't ask old people to get across a creek even if it was clear weather. We got permission from the farmer to go through his property, after a lot of help from interested people.

We set the date for the service at Ramahyuck and invitations were sent out to people we thought would like to be present. The papers called it the Pilgrimage to Ramahyuck. Well it was. Dark people and white came from everywhere—they say there must have been three hundred or more. Laurie Hamlyn set up bales of hay for seats and it was a wonderful day in memory of Nathaniel Pepper.

Rev. Hagenauer's granddaughters were with us and we got talking and we remembered my Dad Percy used to go and see Rev. Hagenauer's son, who

120

A section of the crowd at the Memorial Service in 1977.

was also a minister, every time he was in Melbourne. That man went to visit the Dad when he was sick in the Repat. Hospital in Melbourne. 'Course they were both kids together at the mission school.

Then there was Rev. Bulmer's granddaughter, Brenda Hoffman. She told us how old John Bulmer used to come down from Lake Tyers to hold services at Ramahyuck, and that's right. Her Dad and my Dad worked together strippin' bark. The two old missionary men were good friends and the Aborigines loved them both.

Rev. Hahn's two grandsons were there and had some photos to show us of the pupils at the Ramahyuck school.

We had three pastors from the Aboriginal Evangelical Fellowship: Ossie Cruse, who is Nathaniel's great-grandson, Neville Lilley and Tommy Coe. Neville started the service off with a hymn. Then I told the people a bit about Nathaniel, how he left off a hundred years ago and what's following along after him now with our Christian brothers and sisters throughout Australia.

Tommy Kirk works for the Archaeological Survey and he talked on the importance of preserving any Aboriginal relics, the canoe trees, toe-hold trees and things like that.

Bruce Evans, the M.P., told the people we had gathered in a very historic and 'very hallowed spot' for a very special occasion:

'We must try to cast our minds back to the scene that may have been here and try and conjure up in our minds what this place was like a hundred years ago, on the day Nathaniel Pepper was buried in the cemetery at Ramahyuck, and it is very difficult, I find, when looking at the surroundings here to conjure up what life was like in those days. When we think of the whole concept of Ramahyuck which was an Aboriginal Mission Station, in the same style as Lake Tyers was up to a few years ago . . . I would think it is reasonable to assume that the early Christian people in this country, seeing that the white settlers had taken over the traditional hunting grounds of the Aboriginal people, could see that unless something was done to meet their physical needs, their needs for food and shelter, that they must eventually perish. If the white man has taken away all his traditional hunting grounds then I think it is reasonable to presume that

121

his best hunting grounds were always those that were most sought after pasturing grounds by the early white settlers.

'. . . One of the factors that is most noticeable in Aboriginal people, I think perhaps one of the factors that has received the least recognition of the lot, is that in their tribal state they had very strong traditional rights and a very strong code of ethics and as we've tried to replace their physical needs, unless we can replace their spiritual needs with something of equal or greater value, then too I think we are faced with a decline, just as we as a group of people in our own country are faced with a decline if we allow our spiritual standards to drift away and be forgotten about. As far as I'm concerned the people amongst the Aboriginal race who have these high spiritual needs satisfied, shine out so much that I think it's a proof in itself among these people as it is proof among our own, that where spiritual values are high then you will see the satisfaction, the concern for other people which is all too important. All too often I think we are concerned with our own requirements and forget about the needs of our community as a whole.

'. . . so we pay tribute to Nathaniel Pepper the first Christian among the Aboriginal people who came here to preach the Gospel, to convert the Aboriginal people in this area, who apparently saw the need to fulfil the spiritual needs which were going to be changed by the course of time, by the new society which had overtaken his people. I'm quite certain in my mind the spirit which Nathaniel Pepper had, has rubbed off over the years, perhaps over the generations to his grandson—Phillip Pepper, to Phillip's own family who are showing the way as far as I can see to their people and I think to many of our people as well. Today I think we can be very proud of the associations we have with Nathaniel Pepper and the Pepper family.'[3]

Bruce Evans gave a special word of thanks to the owner of the property where we came through to get to the cemetery. He explained we had special permission for the day because the other access was by a very difficult track.

Pastors Neville Lilley, Tom Coe and Ossie Cruse with Phillip.

Rev. Norman Cameron from the Presbyterian Church at Stratford outlined the association between Rev. Hagenauer as a Moravian missionary and the Presbyterian Church. He said the Church believed a mission was necessary for the Aborigines 'who were being decimated by white man's diseases and vices and they were a demoralised people and so the Church became more and more concerned that mission work should be begun . . .'

Pastor Tom Coe who works amongst the people in the Gippsland area said, 'I believe without Christ there is no hope for Aborigines, there's no hope for the white man . . . you can have a house, you can have a car, you can have fine clothes but unless the heart is changed you've got nothing . . . the spiritual need has to be fulfilled in the heart and that can only come from the power of God'.

Tommy Kirk said he was pleased to be at Ramahyuck, 'and it give me great pleasure being an Aboriginal and being involved in this sort of thing. Now this is new to me, I'm a Queenslander and I haven't been down in Victoria very long; as far as I am concerned and from what I see here today, this is a Protected Area from the Victorian Archaeological Survey point of view . . . when I go back I will make a report on this to the State Archaeological . . . and report on what Mr Pepper wants done. You can see a scarred tree from here, it's a dead tree with a double scar. Now to remove that tree would cost you two hundred dollars fine or two years in jail . . .'

Pastor Neville Lilley played his guitar and sang 'The Outback of Australia', composed by Pastor Ronny Williams from South Australia. Pastor Williams tells a story of the outback where 'our natives roam' but there is no man in God's service and adds 'we will go before it is too late'.

Pastor Ossie Cruse is the Federal Council Member for the Aboriginal Evangelical Fellowship of Australia and the Chairman of the Lands Trust of New South Wales. He is also the pastor of the church at Eden. He addressed the people:

> *'For all those who participated today, thank you in the name of the Lord. I know there are many people involved in the betterment of the Aboriginal people of Australia and it's good to see so many people represented here. We do have our National representative here Mrs Nessie Skuta . . . there are other members here involved with Aboriginal people . . . I dedicate these closing moments to Nathaniel Pepper and to our Lord and Saviour Jesus Christ . . . The Evangelical Fellowship of Australia is the result of many dedicated persons written down in history. We are the result of missionaries, and I will say this without any fear, that if it had not been for the early missionaries who presented the Gospel message of salvation to our people we would not be here. For this reason then it gives me great pleasure to take part in this Memorial Service, especially then to lift up the One who made it all possible, the Lord Jesus Christ . . . Heavenly Father we can thank you for this day, we thank you for the memory of Nathaniel Pepper, we thank you for what we have heard from the lips of many people; we know there is a growing concern for the destiny of the Aboriginal people; . . . Father we pray that you will be with us, give us guidance and direction and especially give us wisdom . . .'[4]*

Fr Joseph Butscher was with us too and he spoke to the people about what the Aborigines in Western Australia are doing and how they work on the

Phillip, Ethel, Sarah Cruse (neé Pepper), Dora Green (neé Pepper) and Pastor Ossie Cruse, March 1977.

missions there. At one place they've got a soft drink factory, and they make the drink and sell it in the towns. At another place they grow vegetables and sell them. The trouble is me tape run out before he was having his talk and I didn't know, so I can't write it here, all he said to us. He's a farmer and he knows about the ground and what it can produce, that's why he was interested in Lake Tyers and in the people and he knows that for Aborigines to make a go of these things they have got to be trained for it.

At the end of the Memorial Service Rev. Hagenauer's granddaughter said she was thinking all the time about how over a hundred years ago our grandfathers had such a shining faith and that it was something she felt we can't hold a candle to, but we just have to keep on trying. And she was right.

Well, after we left Ramahyuck everyone was invited to go to Knob Reserve in Stratford where a barbecue lunch was provided by the Shire and the Historical Society and a lot of people. They had meat, cakes, sandwiches, tea and plenty of it—they put on a great turn. The Historical Society had pictures and artifacts on show and the people all joined in to make my grandfather's day one to remember. As people like the Aboriginal parsons, the Presbyterian minister, a Catholic priest, Mr Alan West—he's one of those anthropologists—Members of Parliament, the television people, the dark people and the white people all mixed together, I reckon everyone got to know more about Aborigines and I hope that will help friendship.

I want to see the cemetery made an official one, to protect the remains of those buried there, forever. Part of Ramahyuck, or a place near, could be set up as a memorial to our people and tourists could go and see how and where the Aborigines lived. If the Shire could fetch a road along and put in toilets and a barbecue area, tourists could come and, if they wanted to, they could throw a line into the Avon for a feed of fish.

EAST GIPPSLAND REGIONAL
PLANNING COMMITTEE

Marion Le Cheminant is involved in fieldwork for an inventory of 'historical features of conservation significance' for the East Gippsland Regional Planning Committee. She writes:

> *'The Ramahyuck cemetery is an important historical site in East Gippsland. It should be given proper recognition and care and I would like to personally support the efforts of the people who are endeavouring to restore it.*

> *'Recently I carried out a survey of historical sites and features in East Gippsland for the East Gippsland Regional Planning Committee. It was a moving and unforgettable experience to have been there in March 1977 when a commemoration and thanksgiving ceremony was held on the centenary of Nathaniel Pepper's death.*

> *'It is important to remember that many, many Aborigines were buried in this place, during a particular period in our history. People need such places to remind them of the reality of the past; we should not deny that need to future generations.'*[5]

In Victoria we have got two members of the National Aboriginal Conference and Nessie Skuta is one. She lives in Gippsland and she understands about Ramahyuck and is willing to help us in any way she can.

In them early days they reckoned the Aborigines would all die out and thousands of our people did. Just in Gippsland alone there were over 2000 Kurnai and that's a lotta blackfellas. That was before Angus McMillan come here. By the time Rev. John Bulmer and Rev. Hagenauer rescued our mob, there were 250.*

Now you know why we want Ramahyuck cared for. At least we know where some of our ancestors are buried.

---

* Angus McMillan was in Gippsland in 1840. John Bulmer went to Buchan in 1860, Rev. Hagenauer followed in 1862.

Our Golden Wedding Anniversary

OUR GOLDEN WEDDING

WELL WE GOT AN INVITATION FOR THE 'BACK TO NEWMERELLA' DO AND o'course we went. I told you before Ethel's family lived there and Ethel went to the first school they had on the flats. When we got married at Newmerella we lived there too. Joe De Piazza was my best man and a good friend all these years. He had a shop not far from where we lived. Our wedding anniversary was in March 1978 and poor old Joe died a few months later.

They had this surprise party for us and they had a big cake too and we never knew about that until it happened. They kept it a good secret, eh? The *Snowy River Mail* wrote a bit about us and took a photo for the paper. That party made us real happy. We met our old friends and everybody had a good time and one bloke called out 'You're real *nuc-car-gn*'; that means a real flash person—see they were havin' a go at us. We had a lot of laughs.

We got a letter from Peter Nixon and I don't reckon he'd mind me putting it in here. After all, we've known his family a long time and the Aborigines of Gippsland and our own relations worked on the ground for his old grandfather and they've been pretty decent to the Aborigines.

Ethel and Phillip cutting the Golden Wedding Anniversary cake.

Ethel playing the piano.

Minister For Transport,
Orbost.
10 April 1978

Mr and Mrs Phil Pepper

Dear Phil,

I wish to convey to you both my personal congratulations on the recent celebration of your Golden Wedding Anniversary.

The 'Surprise Party' held recently at Newmerella was an occasion for your many friends to share your happiness, and I have no doubt that the event brought you great joy.

As lifetime residents of East Gippsland you will have witnessed numerous changes, and I am sure could re-tell many interesting stories of the past.

May I take this opportunity to commend you and your wife on your personal contributions to the community in this area.

Wishing you many years of happiness together.

Yours sincerely,

Peter Nixon

The original Pepper family home at the Swamp, 1979.

Well a bit of a while after our wedding anniversary, we thought it would be a good idea to have a look at some of the changes, so I went back to Koo-wee-rup with Ethel on Melbourne Cup Day of 1979. I wanted to see Dad's old house and property at the Swamp—to see the places where we worked, to take a look at where Ethel and meself took the family to live during the Depression —and I wanted to look up some old mates too. We just jumped in the car and headed off to the Swamp, with no arrangements made to meet anybody, just to poke around a bit.

Fifty-five years ago, the following article appeared in the Koo-wee-rup *Sun:*

> *'The Swamp developed and graduated to Bunyip South and later Iona, Cora Lynn, Modella (or Mudella as it was more aptly called) and Vervale, but to those who saw it in its early stages it is still the Swamp, and those higher sounding names are merely used as a form of postal address.'*[1]

When we got to Cardinia we saw Matt Killeen's Soldier Settlement block where I camped and dug spuds for Dick O'Hare. Dixon's block reminded me how Jack and Hilda Dixon left the swamp and went to the Police Paddocks, how we rode our horses, Sammy and me, from the Swamp to see them. Then there was Gile's block, the top class farmer, and the others whose names I still remember.

It was a pretty movin' thing goin' back there after all these years. Anyway the owners said I could take a walk around the place and I did. They told me the attachment was still in the ceiling roof where we had a kero lantern hung

Then, when we reached our block where our old house still stands, I could see the place had hardly changed over the years except the front was ploughed up where we had a garden. The old dairy is still there but the Italians who own it now have made it into a wash-house. We had two big water tanks at the side of the house. Looking at that old house brought back memories of the past. I walked down the drive beside the old scraggy pine trees and round the back of the house. The people there were very nice and when I told them who I was they offered me some vino and home made cheese. I wasn't keen on that and this Italian gave me a glass of beer.

that we rolled up and down when we needed it, and the boards were still fixed to the walls that were stuck there to keep out the draughts when the wood shrunk over fifty years ago.

I thought of Dad goin' crook about that draught, and the twenty odd years later when he was sick in Melbourne and they sent word to me at Orbost and we went down and stayed for three days with him. He died not long after. As I walked from the side of the old three bedroomed weatherboard to the front, I kept thinkin' of Mum dying there in 1924. It's a long time. I could see the little old flower garden, cosmos to the roadway she had, and roses across the front. Then there was the old violet patch she had growin' and dahlias in bloom. None of them was really there, but I could see them easy. Even the vegies growing at the side of the house paddock to save her runnin' down the back paddock for spuds and things.

I sat down on the front steps where I'd sat so long ago with my brother Sam and my sisters watching the flood water creep up higher. There was the spot where Sam and me stood with our long pants rolled up to our knees just in front of the house.

There's only three of us left now and I'd have liked to have had my sisters Dora and Sarah with me that day. You know when you're going over fifty odd years in your mind you keep thinkin' of things like Dad telling us to put lawn in the front, but Mum sayin' she wanted flowers . . . the floods, losing everything and startin' again . . . the good times and the bad. I remembered all the great neighbours we had on the other Soldier Settlement blocks who most went broke and had to walk out like us. Some stayed on and descendants live there at the Swamp. The sports days everyone went to. 'Course the floods don't reach our ground now, this Italian said.

Phillip on the homestead verandah.

We drove into the town lookin' for any people my age but couldn't see any so I went into a shop that was there in my day to ask if the shopkeeper knew any of my friends. A woman come in and I said to her, 'Now you're a senior citizen and you might be able to help me.' I asked if she was one of the old identities and she was. I said I had lived at the swamp many years ago and she woke up who I was. She would have been a schoolgirl when I knew her and her brothers Clem and Ivan Loveday. Clem was in their car outside and they invited us to their home for a cuppa tea and we had a great yarn there. We even saw the Melbourne Cup on their telly. They gave me all the news about the old soldiers who had blocks around the swamp with Dad's and I found out one of my bike rider friends Percy Osborne was in the Dandenong hospital. The old pub in the town is still there where they had the spud tallies in the early days. I know one bloke could dig fifty bags there in a day, others got their twenties and thirties. I could do thirty but me tally never went up in the pub because I didn't drink and never went in. There are buildings in the town now where there was just paddocks when we lived there.

Since that day I've met another of my friends, Tom Burhop. They were on a block, same as us, and he had photos of the old swamp. We had a great talk together:

> *'Your sisters and Sammy were at school with me, but I remember Lena and Sammy the most. You were working on the farm then. Sammy was a bright boy but he hated school. All he ever wanted was to be out in the bush. Do you remember your poor old Dad coming to school with Sam, with a whip? Poor old Percy had terrible trouble to get Sammy to school and many times we would see them arrive at the school gates, Percy*

Phillip's family during the 1940s. *(left to right) Front:* **Gwen, Dora, Phillip.** *Back:* **Les Green, Percy Pepper, Sammy and his wife, Maud, and Alice** (Stratford Historical Society).

Pepper with a whip in his hand. He would never come through the school gates—just stand there and watch to see that Sammy didn't come out. Once in, Sammy would go round the other side of the school, get over the fence and into the scrub. It was easy enough to disappear there as the bush was about nine feet high. Sammy would wag school for days, happy in the bush, usually bird-nesting, and Percy would get landed with a two pound fine. Sammy knew so much about the bush he was great fun to be with. He was bright in school but he was happier with his boomerang and shanghai in his hand. He was never without them at school.

'How about those boomerangs you made? Sammy used to bring one to school every now and then and tell us you made it. We had about a dozen at one time, all lined up on the top ledge of the blackboard. He brought a big one to school once, but it was cracked. You'd knocked it into some rocks and it was in bad shape so we patched it up and used it. We had great fun with your boomerangs at school. Then one year when we went back to school after the holidays, they were all gone. The teacher had taken the lot.'[2]

How d'you like that? After 53 years I find out it was Sammy pinchin' my boomerangs. I always thought the old man was giving them away. He had a habit of giving things away. Those boomerangs kept disappearing and I kept making them and Sammy kept pinchin' them for school.

I'd like to finish this book with these words that I learnt a long long time ago.

> Little drops of water, little grains of sand
> God joined them all together
> And made this a glorious land.

Dalmore East State School attended by the Percy Pepper children. *(left to right)* *Front:* Cliff Woods, Wilfred Levey, _____ Hogan, Orm White, Stan McGowan. *Centre:* Annie Woods, Lena Pepper, Tom Burhop, Bob Petters, _____ Hogan. *Back:* Pauline Giles, Bessie Giles, Rose Levey, Gwen Pepper, Clare Woods, _____, Sam Pepper. Teacher, E. Elliott, January 1923 (Tom Burhop).

Ramahyuck Preserved

Part of the Cemetery with the high land in the background, December 1979 (Dr Josephine Flood).

IN 1862 A CROWN ROAD RESERVE WAS DECLARED AND SURVEYORS DIRECTÉD the access route to the Cemetery over a creek which had a spring in its bed. From the establishment of the mission until 1900, Aborigines and white people ignored this track and passed across the Ramahyuck property on the high ground. Their right to the Cemetery was never challenged.

Geoff Hahn recalls that as a schoolboy it was customary to have 'bird days' and, as the excursions were along the creek past the Cemetery, the students were given an outline of the historical importance of the area. In the spring the Cemetery was a mass of colour with flowering freesias, jonquils and bella-donna lilies and the wooden crosses were dotted throughout the whole fenced area. A few of the marble stones could be seen through the kangaroo grass. During the Gippsland fires of 1943 some of the crosses were destroyed and part of the fence, but Roy Marshall, the adjoining land-owner, re-fenced the Cemetery at his own cost. Early in 1950 the land changed hands and 'soon after some people learned with dismay that all trace of a fence round the Cemetery had gone and stock grazed over this sacred land . . .'

In 1976 a renewed interest was taken in the Cemetery by Phillip. Wishing to have the area preserved in a fitting manner and to have access to it, he sought the assistance of the Avon Shire Council, the Ministry of Conservation and the Department of Aboriginal Affairs. As a result a Committee of Management was appointed; their task 'is to preserve, reinstate and maintain

The ruins of the Baum gravestone and the fenceless Cemetery.

The Committee of Management for the Cemetery in front of a scarred tree at Howitt's Park, Bairnsdale. *(left to right)* G. Hahn, P. Pepper, N. Skuta, L. Hamlyn, J. Stewart (Committee of Management).

Dr Josephine Flood with Phillip (Bairnsdale Advertiser).

the Cemetery and to make it possible for relatives and historians to visit the Cemetery if they so desire.'

In response to requests made by Phillip concerning the protection of the sacred and historical Ramahyuck area, Dr Flood, Senior Conservation Officer for the Australian Heritage Commission, visited the Burial Ground in December 1979. Dr Flood believes the Cemetery is well deserving of preservation and notice of intention to enter Ramahyuck Cemetery Reserve in the Register of the National Estate appeared in the Melbourne *Age*, 26 February 1980.

In April 1980 Senator Chaney, Minister of Aboriginal Affairs, advised Phillip that the approval of the adjoining land-owner had been obtained to

A toe-hold tree at Ramahyuck. This tree is on the track into the Cemetery and the toe holds were cut by Kurnai tribesmen with stone axes. There are a number of these trees in the Gippsland district. Such trees are rare in many parts of Australia and are an important part of Australian Aboriginal history (Dr Josephine Flood).

bridge the creeks. In reply, Phillip stated that he was looking for wheel access over the high land:

'. . . not what was suggested by white men—access over the creeks. You see our people and the white people crossed over the high land to the cemetery and never got their feet wet . . . It is wheel access I am asking for, and have been asking for, for a long time now . . . let anyone go in where they always did, and then white people too can see how our poeple lived. They could see important scarred trees along the river and other places too.

'Politicians are all talking about saving our sacred sites and relics. Well Ramahyuck has all that and I will not stop asking you and everyone else I think can help me preserve this place. I am not getting any younger and I am worried about this place. It is a great way to teach people about the Aborigines and this is what all the talk about is in Parliament now.

'. . . After all, that ground was my own relations' land and the English laws took it away from them. One white man, Mr Kuch, sits on it now.

The legal track from the Cemetery through one of the creeks.

> *My people, my own blood relations are in that ground at the cemetery. I want to be able to go in the right way, not have to sneak along and across a creek.*

> *'I am not asking for all that ground back where our people lived on the mission station. All I want is a bit of ground where it is on high land and it has got to be for wheel access.*

> *'Will you please listen to me Senator? Will you please come to Gippsland and see for yourself? Aborigines all over Australia are asking for their own ground to be given back. All I am asking for is what is rightfully what belongs to our people and those others who want to know and learn about Aborigines, can go there . . .'*

Senator Chaney informed Phillip of fencing which had been carried out on the Cemetery Reserve:

> *'Mr Kuch has run his stock over the remains of my people long enough and I thank you for the fence to protect that site. If you could do that for my people when nobody else could, then I know you can do more. I will rest when I know I can go to the cemetery over the high land, the proper way.'*

Note to Second Edition. Laurie Hamlyn, Geoff Hahn and Jim Stewart, members of the committee, were instrumental in building a concrete walkover across the creek connecting the low lying Crown Land to the cemetery side of the hill. Phillip Pepper did not visit Ramahyuck Cemetery, as he wished, 'over the high land'.

Appendix

IN THE LEGISLATIVE ASSEMBLY 12 MARCH 1980 THE BILL TO AMEND THE Archaeological and Aboriginal Relics Preservation Act 1972, the Ministry for Conservation Act 1972, and the National Museum of Victoria Council Act 1972 was read for the first time.

> 'In 1972, Parliament enacted an Archaeological and Aboriginal Relics Pre-servation Act which was designed to afford protection to Aboriginal relics within this State. The purpose of the Bill before the House is to remove some anomalies and to correct some errors which have become evident as a result of our experience with this legislation and to make changes which have become necessary as a consequence of the transfer of the legislation from the Chief Secretary to the Minister for Conservation.

> '. . . It is the hope of the Government that the protection of our archaeo-logical sites will provide the key to the understanding of the beginnings of aboriginal life in Victoria and promote a greater interest within the community in the history of the first Australians.'

In 1974, a submission of the Victorian Government to the national inquiry in Canberra states in reference to Victoria:

> 'Hundreds of aboriginal sites are being destroyed annually (in one State only) by real estate developers both in urban and rural areas, often unknowingly and sometimes with indifference.'

The anomalies and errors referred to in the Bill are known and recognised by a number of Aborigines in Victoria and the presence and protests of a group in the House when debate about the Bill was in progress brought about discussions with Members of Parliament. The outcome of consultation with the Minister of Conservation, Mr W. V. Houghton, resulted in amendments to the Bill. One of the clauses objected to by the Aborigines was in respect to the rights of a Minister to declare a site to be of no archaeological importance or significance. Mr Houghton decided that this will be done only after consultation with the Archaeological and Aboriginal Relics Advisory Com-mittee. The fine previously set at $200 for destruction of relics and relic sites is now increased to $1000. The number of Aboriginal members on this committee of twelve persons was increased from two to three. At least one of the members of the Legislative Council stated that three people from the Aboriginal community were not enough to have on the committee. The Aboriginal spokesman would have liked more than three. Mr Houghton later said he did not intend to be inflexible in the future about that proposition.

A canoe tree on the Avon River destroyed by fire, 1979.

The Melbourne *Sun*, 2 May 1980, reported:

> *'The Bill now provides that anyone may have access to a relic site by application to the Conservation Minister.*
>
> *'And the Minister must now consult the advisory committee before declaring relics.'*

Tess De Araugo,
Melbourne

References

Chapter 1: Nathaniel of the Wotjoballuk Tribe
1 (a) 'Further Facts Relating to the Moravian Mission', numbers 1 and 2. The La Trobe Collection, State Library of Victoria.
  (b) 'Periodical Accounts of the Moravian Mission'. Courtesy Miss S. Robertson, Melbourne.
  (c) Report of the Select Committee appointed by the Victorian Parliament to inquire into Aboriginal welfare, 1858–1859.
2 (a) Todd, A., Diary. The La Trobe Collection, State Library of Victoria.
  (b) Todd, A., Letter to the Melbourne *Age*, 5 June 1884.
3 *The Victorian Historical Magazine*, vol. IV, March 1915.
4 Port Phillip Association Papers. The La Trobe Collection, State Library of Victoria.
5 Gellibrand, J. T., 'Memoranda of a Trip to Port Phillip in 1836'. The La Trobe Collection, State Library of Victoria.
6 Lonsdale, W., Correspondence. Public Record Office, Victoria.
7 Lonsdale, W., Correspondence.
8 First Report of the Central Board Appointed to Watch over the Interests of the Aborigines in the Colony of Victoria, 1861. The La Trobe Collection, State Library of Victoria.
9 (a) Thomas, W., 'Select Committee of Enquiry into the Condition of the Aborigines, 1847'. The La Trobe Collection, State Library of Victoria.
  (b) Report of the Select Committee on the Aborigines and Protectorate, New South Wales, Votes and Proceedings, 1849 (1849) vol. 2. The La Trobe Collection, State Library of Victoria.
  (c) La Trobe, C. J., Letterbooks, Public Record Office, Victoria.
10 (a) Victorian Legislative Council Votes and Proceedings, 1858–1859. The La Trobe Collection, State Library of Victoria.
  (b) Belcher, G., Diary. The La Trobe Collection, State Library of Victoria.
  (c) Taylor, W., in Bride, T. F. (ed.), *Letters From Victorian Pioneers*, Melbourne, 1898.
  (d) 'Further Facts Relating to the Moravian Mission', 1860–1865, numbers 1–4. The La Trobe Collection, State Library of Victoria.
  (e) Reports of the Central Board Appointed to Watch over the Interests of the Aborigines in the Colony of Victoria, 1861–1864. The La Trobe Collection, State Library of Victoria.
  (f) Gribble, Rev. J., *Black But Comely*, London, 1884.
11 'Moravian Mission to Australia'. Courtesy Rev. Swanston, Melbourne.
12 (a) Hutton, Rev. J., *History of the Moravian Mission.* The La Trobe Collection, State Library of Victoria.
  (b) Moravian Missionary Reports supplied by Mr C. Schooling, Moravian Church House, London.
  (c) Moravian Missionary Reports supplied by Rev. F. Linyard, Moravian Church House, London.
  (d) Minutes of the Central Board Appointed to Watch over the Interests of the Aborigines in the Colony of Victoria. Australian Archives, Melbourne (B314. 1870–1872).
  (e) Chauncy, P., Anecdotes in Smyth, R. B., *The Aborigines of Victoria*, vol. 2, Melbourne, Government Printer, 1878.

13 (a) *The Aborigines of Victoria.*
   (b) Information per correspondence supplied by Rev. J. Brown, Western Australia.
   (c) Information per correspondence supplied by Miss Bonnie Hicks, Western Australia.
   (d) Information per correspondence supplied by Miss Margaret Medcalf, Western Australia.
   (e) J. S. Battye Library of West Australian History, Perth, Western Australia.
   (f) Minutes of the Central Board Appointed to Watch over the Interests of the Aborigines in the Colony of Victoria. Australian Archives, Melbourne (B314. 1870–1872).

Chapter 2: Nathaniel in Gippsland
1 (a) Bulmer, Rev. J., Collection. National Museum, Victoria.
   (b) Ramahyuck Correspondence Files, 1863. Australian Archives, Melbourne (B313).
2 School Inspector's Report, Ramahyuck Mission Station School. Courtesy J. Hahn, Maffra, Victoria.
3 Hagenauer, Rev. F. A., 'Mission Work Among the Aborigines of Victoria', Melbourne, 1880. The La Trobe Collection, State Library of Victoria.
4 (a) 'Mission Work Among the Aborigines of Victoria'.
   (b) Ramahyuck Correspondence File. Australian Archives, Melbourne (B313. 1860–1880).
5 Translation from unknown German magazine dated 1877. Courtesy Dr L. Grope, President of the Lutheran Church of Australia 1979.

Chapter 3: The Act and its Effect
1 (a) Reports of the Central Board Appointed to Watch over the Interests of the Aborigines in the Colony of Victoria, 1861–1869. The La Trobe Collection, State Library of Victoria.
   (b) Lake Condah Correspondence File. Australian Archives, Melbourne (B313. 1867–1884).
   (c) Outward Correspondence written by the Secretary of the Central Board for the Protection of Aborigines, 1885–1889. Australian Archives, Melbourne (B329).
   (d) Acts and Regulations, 1879–1957. Australian Archives, Melbourne (B313).
2 Robinson, G., Report to Superintendent C. La Trobe, 1844, on his journey into south-eastern Australia. Public Record Office, Melbourne.
3 Outward Correspondence written by the Secretary of the Central Board for the Protection of Aborigines, 1896. Australian Archives, Melbourne (B329).
4 General Correspondence File, 1896. Australian Archives, Melbourne (B313).
5 Ramahyuck (Lake Wellington) Correspondence File. Australian Archives, Melbourne (B313. 1905).

Chapter 4: The Last Tribal War
1 (a) Bulmer, Rev. J., Collection, Royal Historical Society of Victoria, Melbourne.
   (b) Bulmer, Rev. J., Collection, National Museum, Victoria.
2 Bulmer, Rev. J., Collection, National Museum, Victoria.
3 Bulmer, Rev. J., Collection, National Museum, Victoria.
4 Bulmer, Rev. J., Collection, National Museum, Victoria.

Chapter 5: An Aboriginal is
1 Tyers, C. J., Journal, Mitchell Library, Sydney, New South Wales.
2 Cameron, J., in 'Early Days of Orbost', from *Personalities and Stories of the Early Orbost District* collected by Mary Gilbert, B.E.M., 1972.
3 Geoff Hahn is the grandson of Rev. Heinrich Hahn, Moravian missionary at Ramahyack 1875.

Chapter 6: Grandfather Billy Thorpe
1 Bulmer, Rev. J., Collection, National Museum, Victoria.
2 (a) Lake Condah Correspondence File, 1885–1904. Australian Archives, Melbourne (B313).
   (b) Outward Correspondence written by the Secretary of the Central Board for the Protection of Aborigines, 1885–1904. Australian Archives, Melbourne (B329).
3 *Weekly Times*, Melbourne, 16 February 1896.

Chapter 7: The 1914–18 War
1 Coulthard-Clark, G. D., 'Aboriginal Medal Winners', *Australian Army Journal*, March 1973.

Chapter 8: After the War

1 The Koo-wee-rup *Sun*, 20 December 1923.
2 The Koo-wee-rup *Sun*, 19 October 1922.
3 The Koo-wee-rup *Sun*, 22 February 1923.
4 The Koo-wee-rup *Sun*, 24 July 1924.
5 The Koo-wee-rup *Sun*, 23 July 1925.
6 (a) Annual Reports of the Central Board Appointed to Watch over the Interests of the Aborigines in the Colony of Victoria presented to Parliament, 1861–1955. The La Trobe Collection, State Library of Victoria.
   (b) Bulmer, Rev. J., Collection, National Museum, Victoria.
7 (a) History Section, Education Department, Victoria.
   (b) Minutes of the Central Board for the Protection of Aborigines, 1901. Australian Archives, Melbourne (B333).
8 (a) Population Statistics, Correspondence File, 1863. Australian Archives, Melbourne (B312).
   (b) Lands and Surveys, Correspondence File, 1861–1895. Australian Archives, Melbourne (B313).
   (c) Lake Tyers Correspondence File, inward correspondence, 1876–1896. Australian Archives, Melbourne (B356).

Chapter 9: Living on or off a Reserve

1 Minutes of the Central Board for the Protection of Aborigines, 1872–1894. Australian Archives, Melbourne (B315).
2 (a) Census and Statistics, 1879–1957. Australian Archives, Melbourne (B313).
   (b) Aborigines Protection Act 1886.
   (c) Minutes of the Central Board for the Protection of Aborigines, 1907–1921. Australian Archives, Melbourne (B315).
3 (a) Lake Tyers Correspondence File, Administration, 1920–1958. Australian Archives, Melbourne (B356).
   (b) Lake Tyers Correspondence File, Managers' Reports, 1918–1930. Australian Archives, Melbourne (B356).
   (c) Outward Correspondence written by the Secretary of the Central Board for the Protection of Aborigines, 1920–1922. Australian Archives, Melbourne (B329).

Chapter 10: Managers at Lake Tyers

1 (a) Lake Tyers Correspondence File, Staff, 1904–1933. Australian Archives, Melbourne (B356).
   (b) Lake Tyers Correspondence File, Managers' Reports, 1933. Australian Archives, Melbourne (B356).

Chapter 11: Depression Days

1 The Bairnsdale *Advertiser*, 25 September 1934.
2 The Bairnsdale *Advertiser*, 13 July 1934.
3 The Bairnsdale *Advertiser*, 5 January 1934.
4 The Bairnsdale *Advertiser*, 12 January 1934.
5 (a) Lake Tyers Correspondence File, Managers' Report, 1934. Australian Archives, Melbourne (B346).
   (b) Minutes of the Central Board for the Protection of Aborigines, 1928–1938. Australian Archives, Melbourne (B315).

Chapter 12: Lake Tyers Portraits

1 Leason, P., Portraits, State Library of Victoria, Melbourne.
2 Minutes of the Central Board for the Protection of Aborigines, 1934. Australian Archives, Melbourne (B315).
3 The Bairnsdale *Advertiser*, 30 October 1934.

Chapter 13: From Under the Rule at Lake Tyers

1 The Bairnsdale *Advertiser*, 29 January 1974.
2 (a) *The Victorian Year Book 1973*.
   (b) *Lake Tyers Land Title* (Booklet), Ministry of Aboriginal Affairs, Melbourne, 1971.

Chapter 14: The Australian Aboriginal Vote

1 (a) Interviews conducted by researcher and documents held by the author.
  (b) As recorded in *Hansard* (Senate), 31 July 1974.
2 *The Victorian year Book 1973.*
3 The Melbourne *Herald*, 9 July 1974.
4 (a) The Bairnsdale *Advertiser*, 18 July 1974.
  (b) 27 July 1974.
5 Correspondence held by author.

Chapter 15: As We Are

1 Department of Aboriginal Affairs.
2 (a) Lake Boga Collection, Royal Historical Society of Victoria, Melbourne.
  (b) *Mission Success Among the Aborigines*, Victorian Religious Pamphlets, 1860. The La Trobe Collection, State Library of Victoria.
  (c) Lands and Surveys, Correspondence File, 1861–1895. Australian Archives, Melbourne (B313).
  (d) Outward Correspondence written by the Secretary of the Central Board for the Protection of Aborigines, 1890–1897. Australian Archives, Melbourne (B329).
3 (a) Annual Reports presented to Parliament, 1871–1906. Australian Archives, Melbourne (B333).
  (b) Aborigines Protection Act 1886, Acts and Regulations, 1879–1957. Australian Archives, Melbourne (B313).

Chapter 16: Ramahyuck

1 Crown Lands Department, Melbourne.
2 Correspondence held by author.
3 Taped recordings held by author.
4 Taped recordings held by author.
5 Correspondence held by author.

Chapter 17: Our Golden Wedding Anniversary

1 The Koo-wee-rup *Sun*, July 1924.
2 Burhop, T., interview.

Kurnai Vocabulary

The words and phrases used in the text by Phillip Pepper have been written down as nearly as possible in the way in which he pronounces them. Many of the words sound the same as those recorded by Rev. John Bulmer and Rev. F. A. Hagenauer over one hundred years ago. The spelling of language recorders varies. As the different groups of the Kurnai people had their own languages, we have chosen the words and phrases used by Phillip's forebears and those which have been handed down to him.

Parts of the body

cheeks	*wa-ang*
chin	*yain*
ear	*woor-ring*
elbows	*jill ung*
eye	*mre*
fat	*warne wan*
finger nails	*tagera-bret*
flesh	*wor-ri a tang*
foot	*ja-an*
hair	*lit*
hand	*bret*
head	*brook*
liver	*wall-ow-alack*
mouth	*kaat*
stomach	*bullon*
teeth	*ngirrndock*
throat	*tull-lit*
tongue	*jilline*

Place names

Bairnsdale	*Wy-yung*	Type of duck
Cape Conran	*Kerlip* or *Murrow-gunnie*	A corner
Coranderrk Aboriginal Station, Healesville	*Coranderrk*	Christmas tree
Creeks, Boggy	*Narka kowera*	A kind of flint found there
____Cobbannah (enters Mitchell River)	*Booloot*	Type of gum scrub
____Dead-horse (enters Tambo River near Ramrod Creek)	*Gurrun-gurrun-yarn*	Very little water
____Iguana	*Callad-euru*	Red Gum
____Merrijig (east of Mitchell River)	*Nunga-bruggu-la*	A rock through which the wind blows
____Merriman's	*Dur'lin*	
	Boung-warl	
____Stony	*Lane glan*	An edible root
____Swift's	*Bunjura gingee mungee*	

———Tom's	*Warrigallac*	
———Upper Boggy	*Taloo-lumbruck*	A tadpole
Eagle Point	*Nur-rung*	Moon
Ewing's Morass	*Ya yung*	Morass
Grant	*Poork-poork-gill-yarn*	Head of the water
Hills, Castle	*Browit-dar-darnda*	Always snow there
———Quackmungee (near Dargo?)	*Kou-ark-mungee*	Laughing jackass
Jones' Bay	*Dahduck*	Tail of the lake
Lakes, Bunga	*Wurndoang*	Salty lake
———King	*Narran*	Moon
———Reeves	*Walmunyee'ra*	Shallow lake
———Victoria	*Toonal'look*	Long narrow water
———Wellington	*Murla*	A clay found in the lake
Lindenow	*Moor-murn*	
Mossiface	*Marlung-dun*	Mussel-shell
Mounts, Baldhead (east of Wentworth River)	*Tarl-darn*	A little snow
———Howitt	*Toot-buck-culluck*	
———Taylor and Lookout (prominent hills north-west of Bairnsdale)	*Bullung-warl*	Two spears
———Willie (Nowa Nowa north of Lake Tyers)	*Nowr-nowr*	
Raymond Island	*Gragin*	Stony island
Rivers, Aberfeldy	*Nambruc*	Plenty of black possums
———Albert	*Lurt'bit*	
———Avon	*Dooyeedang*	
———Brodribb	*Wrak thun balluk*	Place of gum trees
———Crooked	*Nailung*	Plenty of water-hens
———La Trobe	*Durt'yowan*	Finger
———Macalister	*Wirnwirndook'yeerung*	Song of a bird
———Mitchell	*Wahyang*	Spoon-billed duck
———Nicholson	*Dart'yung*	Root of a water plant
———Perry	*Goomballa*	Climbing
———Snowy (lower areas near sea)	*Karang gil*	Great quantities of water weed
(east bank at mouth)	*Murloo*	
(west side)	*Mardgee-long*	
———Tambo	*Ber'rawan*	
(at mouth)	*Gwannung-bourn*	
(near Tongio)	*Tongio memial*	
———Tarra	*Blindit'yin*	
———Thomson	*Carrang-carrang*	Brackish water
———Wentworth	*Daberda'bara*	Rocky bank
———Wongungarra (joins Wonnangatta River west of Dargo)	*Gwannam-r-rook*	Eaglehawk
———Wonnangatta	*Wontwun*	
Sarsfield	*Turt-toong*	
Straits	*Boollum-boollum*	Ti-trees
Swan Reach	*Wook-gook*	A mopoke (boobook owl)
Tongio Gap	*Mungobabba*	
Yellow Water-holes	*Wath*	A shrimp

Religion

bunyip	*tooridin*
bad spirits	*mur-raage*
evil spirit, 'hairy man'	*nargun*
pointing the bone	*nur-ritch*
taking away the kidney fat	*nur-ritch-bun*
sorcerer	*bugheen*
sorcerer's power to take life	*kooloot*

WILDLIFE
animals

bandicoot	*min-nack*
dingo	*merrigarn*
kangaroo	*jirrah*
koala (native bear)	*kullah*
lizard, small	*keratung*
platypus	*barlijan*
seal	*bithowi*
snake, black	*toon yarak*
____red or brown	*thurung*
wallaby	*tharogang*
whale	*baawang*

birds

cockatoo, black	*nganak* or *gama-gama*
____grey	*karan*
crane, white	*tirtgerawan*
duck, black	*wrang*
____musk	*ban*
____teal	*natath*
____wood	*yellan nandik*
emu	*mi owero*
mutton-bird	*bralak*
parrot, blue mountain	*wattat*
____grass	*toon*
pelican	*burran*
quail	*ooro bi gnanang*
robin redbreast	*buluburang*
sand-piper	*kewet-kewet*

Fish

eel	*no-yabg*
flat-head	*brindat*
perch	*tambun*
sea trout	*billin*
shark	*yalmari*

Shell-fish

crab	*krang ilang*
oyster	*koo-n warra*

sea-weed

kelp	*koonthooi*

Other Words

Aborigines	*gunai* or *koorie* or *kurnai*
men or people belonging to the west	*yaktun*
white man	*lohan*
woman	*wookatt*
youngsters	*unyai*
father	*moongan*
mother	*yuccan*
flash person	*nuc-car-gu*
out of his/her mind	*denbin-n-th-brook*
boomerang	*wangin*
club	*kallack* or *nulla-nulla* or *waddy*
spear	*wall*
spear-shield	*bamerook*
meat	*nullee*
hut	*mia-mia*
day	*woo-run*
night	*pook-kun*
star	*brayel*
east	*kar-wi*
north	*be-ara*
south	*tha*
west	*yack*
one	*koo-to-pau*
two	*boolooman*
three	*boolooman batha kootook*
four	*boolooman batha boolung*
yes	*gna*
no	*gnalko*
tall	*wreckel*
short	*tookat a pan*
small quanitity	*tarlitban*
plenty	*ya ill*
many trees	*yail kallack*
mine	*gnetal*
give me	*kana watha*
whose is this?	*gnana lack a dinda*
news	*lare-wnge*
female sweetheart	*megay*
male sweetheart	*mul-lung*